WORDS FOR LIFE

It is the part of the godparents, by their prayers and encouragements, to assist the parents in those duties which are expressed in the grave and forceful words of the printed exhortation, which I commend to their study and attention.

The salvation of this child, like the salvation of us all lies in the infinite life of God, and his inexhaustible kindness; made present to us in our saviour, poured out in his sacrifice, and joined to us by the link of our baptism. To strengthen this link, to open this channel, is the whole purpose of our religion. and in case the claim of God on our own hearts should lose its force — and such is our perversity, it can — he gives us one another. our friends, our children into our keeping. and bids us open ourselves to him, that through us he may come at them. And so, through the love we have to them, he persuades us to love him.

Part of Austin Farrer's manuscript copy of 'Baptism of a Child' (see page 77).

AUSTIN FARRER

Words for Life

Edited by
Charles Conti & Leslie Houlden

First published in Great Britain 1993
Society for Promoting Christian Knowledge
Marylebone Road
London NW1 4DU

British Library Cataloguing-in-Publication Data
A catalogue record for this book is available from the British Library

ISBN 0-281-04644-1

Typeset by Action Typesetting Ltd, Gloucester
Printed in Great Britain by
BPCC Hazells Ltd
Member of BPCC Ltd

Contents

Contents

· Preface

Farrer, it has been said by a prominent theologian, 'was the greatest Anglican thinker of his generation' – and, it would appear, he has sustained that reputation in and for succeeding generations. His earlier posthumous publications included valued collections of philosophical theology (*Reflective Faith*), penetrating essays on Christian doctrine (*Interpretation and Belief*), and exquisite sermons (*The End of Man* and *The Brink of Mystery*). These became the basis of a Farrer renascence, and an international society was formed. Six conferences have now been held – three in the United States and three in England – resulting in several commentaries on Farrer, and helping to make him known to the wider audience he so richly deserves.

Since his death in 1968 the philosophical climate has changed, and Farrer's delicate brand of theism, blending heart and head, has finally come into its own. Here in these meditations is a hint of that metaphysical courage which introduced broader themes in philosophy and was not afraid of giving sound advice. Yet despite the practical advice, one dare not dismiss this pulpiteer as a woolly-minded theologian letting down philosophical standards. Farrer's intellectual power and sheer range of scholarship, when they did not inspire awe or invite serious study, commanded deep respect. Theologians and philosophers alike acknowledged him as one of the most able minds at Oxford this century; and it seems his influence will extend into the next. Some could be clever but not always to the point, Ian Crombie once remarked; others could be on target but not very clever; Farrer was both, clever *and* to the point. Farrer belonged to a generation of scholars now lost.

Reading these sermons after so long has reminded me of the stature of the man behind the words. There is not only a lyrical quality and an elegance which borders on poetic intensity; there is also a genuine humility in his approach to scriptural exegesis. The writer of a profile years ago said Farrer could make an absolute heathen *want* the faith to be true. Yet he achieved authority without being authoritative and was instructive without being dogmatic. He could be inspirational while possessing a sharp edge. He presented important issues in religion in such a way that one could approach them without embarrassment; light things seriously and serious things lightly. Throughout one is aware of the most refined sensibility at work. He did not write as the scribes or reason as the Pharisees, arguing points so fine they got lost in the mass of detail; he wrote with the broad sweep of a prophet's pen combined with the insight of a person who had penetrated the core of what it means to live with an active faith. Helen Oppenheimer, colleague of Farrer's in the Metaphysicals, wrote in *The Hope of Happiness* that the twentieth century has not been without its prophets. She included Farrer with Teilhard de Chardin and Karl Barth. 'But if already these giants are part of history and the spectacles that they gave us to look through are misting up again with everyday steam and grime, there may be scope for a sort of clearing and polishing operation to allow us to look more clearly at what there is to make us happy' – fulfilled as persons. SPCK have, in this collection, given us once again a cleaning agent; but Farrer's language itself fills one with unmitigated joy. It is a pleasure to see him 'happy in the Lord', celebrating the unbounded delight of theological imagery.

It is for this reason Farrer's sermons have stood the test of time. They testify to the sensibilities of a man combining commitment and contentment.

Charles Conti
The University of Sussex

· Introduction:
Farrer the Preacher

Though sometimes reluctant to go, Austin Farrer was much in demand as a visiting preacher. However, when it came to his own pastoral sphere, he did not believe in visiting preachers. He did not care for sermons by celebrities to provide an 'attraction' for young students ('mackerels to catch sprats'). Rather, preaching was part of the pastor's work for his own: to build up in them a coherent pattern of faith and spiritual practice. Anyway, privately and rightly, he knew he could do better himself. So he did not collude with the preachers' trek round universities: perhaps thirty a week at Oxford and Cambridge alone, plodding in from the station, bag of robes in hand, sermon in pocket.

During his twenty-five years as chaplain at Trinity College, Oxford (1935–60), Farrer's practice was as follows. Each Sunday in term-time, he gave a brief homily of a single paragraph ('Farrergraph') at the Eucharist. In the Book of Common Prayer, the sermon comes between the creed and the offertory, and rather than let the congregation sit for the brief period of his utterance, which he read out with no pretence of oratorical address, he kept them standing: he believed it made for alertness, especially first thing in the morning.

Farrer was unusual and ahead of his time in preaching at a said Communion service. But he did not anticipate later developments in his subject matter. As a rule, he made no attempt to gear his words to the theme of the reading for the day, partly for the good reason that the Prayer Book epistles and gospels usually have no common theme. They are in that respect random, the result of various slippings and dislocations over the course of liturgical history. He spoke mostly about the Eucharist itself, seeking to stir devotion that would focus on the sacrament in one way or another. This was because he believed that to be true and wholesome, and in order to correct and warm the souls of his undergraduates, most of whom had come from the dragooned religion of their public schools and should now learn new freedom. In both respects, his policy reflected his own development. In 1952 he published a collection of these eucharistic homilies, filling them out to provide one for each Sunday of the year, and adding an essay on the Body of Christ, under the title *The Crown of the Year* ('Thou crownest the year with thy goodness', Psalm 65). They are doses of concentrated holiness.

For Evensong in his college chapel, he adopted a mixed policy with regard to preaching. On two Sundays out of eight each term, there was indeed a visitor, who might either give stimulating variety or enhance the value set on the normal fare. On two other Sundays, he preached a full-scale sermon. Many of these are to be found in published collections such as *Said or Sung* (1960), *A Celebration of Faith* (1970), *The End of Man* (1973), *The Brink of Mystery* (1976), and now, *Austin Farrer: The Essential Sermons* (SPCK 1991).

On the remaining four Sundays, he gave a briefer,

usually scriptural address. A number of them have survived, and hitherto they have remained unpublished. Now we offer forty of them. As always, they were given from a full script, often written on the back of earlier sermons. Farrer was generous with eloquence but thrifty with paper. Readers may find their length manageable for meditative use, and be glad to have more examples of this master's voice.

Leslie Houlden

1 · Our Father

The Lord's Prayer consists of three hearty wishes, and three humble requests. People greeting one another the world over use expressions which amount to the wish that their friends may have what they want. They wish one another a good morning, or health, or the divine protection. But now we are to greet our heavenly Father; and what can we wish to him, without impertinence? He is our common father — we can at least wish that his name may be honoured by all the family who bear it. He is sovereign king — we may wish for his rule most visibly to prevail. He is a heart of love, full of purpose for his creatures: we may wish that his purposes, just as they are in heaven — that is, in his heavenly mind — may take effect in us here on earth.

By wishing thus, we are simply to give our wills to God, because we love him. And then, because *he* loves *us*, we are bold to make our requests, and these are most simple and most basic: for the provision of material need in all his vast family; for the forgiveness of our sins, our most grudging and unworthy service of so dear a father; and, if it please

1

God, to be spared trials beyond our strength, for fear that we fall into the hands of his enemies and deny him.

Such is the Lord's Prayer, truly terrifying in its simplicity; and which of us can pray it? But then it is the Lord's Prayer; Jesus can pray it: to enter into this prayer is to enter into Christ.

2 · The Words of the Book

There never was a man who had a more overwhelming sense of divine inspiration than St John. The words of his Revelation are dictated to him, he does not write as he chooses. And it is not only that the words come unbidden, even unwelcome, to his pen; he is also aware of a presence, a mighty being with folded pinions and blazing eyes who speaks to him in the very voice of Christ. 'Behold, I come quickly: blessed is he that keepeth the words of the prophecy of this book.' St John falls on his knees in worship. 'No,' says the angel, 'not me. I am, with you and any other prophet, a mouthpiece of God; I am subject, like you, to the truth I speak; I am a fellow-servant to all those who keep the words of this book. Worship God.' Even the angel is the slave of the book; and if St John is to worship anything but God himself, it seems he would do better to worship the book than the angel. Why, but the book is the work of his own hands, he has written it. And what idolatry can be more naïve than to worship what we ourselves have made − an idolatry nevertheless, all too commonly paid to books by the authors of them.

Ah, but St John's book is not an imaginative invention, nor is it a speculative theory. It is the words of God, uttered by Christ and now freshly meditated by St John, and brought alive in him by the action of Christ's Spirit. Here is the book, lying on the writer's desk, with the ink of the last page scarcely dry. He had had a vision, itself recorded on a previous page, of the same book in the right hand of the Almighty, taken by the slaughtered Christ, and opened for us all. And, on a later page, he has recorded how the book came down to him in the hands of the angel, and how he was made to consume it and digest it, so that he could re-express it in spontaneous utterance; and so the book has come out in ink on the papyrus roll which now lies before him. 'Blessed is he, that keepeth the words of the prophecy of this book.' It is the same blessing which Moses gave to Israel of old, when he brought them the statutes, and ordinances, and judgements down from the mountain, that they might keep them and live.

Well, and are there no faults in St John's book, no alloys to the gold, no flaws of human imperfection in the divine transcript? No doubt there are many, but do they affect the practical substance, do they corrupt the text of those words which angels and humans alike must bind themselves to observe? Jesus comes quickly: even if there is no cataclysm, and you or I live as long as old St John, we haven't all the time in the world to spend, refining on the text of God's words: we have to get on with keeping them.

St John is on his knees; his ink is just dry. You are on your knees; you have read the gospel, and prayed; your prayer has just dried in your mouth. What did you pray for? Did you not pray to do the word of Christ, as you have been able, by his Spirit's aid, to understand it, and to apply it to your life? Form the resolution clearly and keep it till you have a better; God may teach you more fully another day, but this is what he says to you now. Was your inspiration, like St John's, brought you by the message of an angel? If so, the invisible and self-effacing messenger falls on his knees beside you and worships the good pleasure of God, expressed in the resolution he teaches you to frame; it is an echo of the will which made the world, and which is set to transform all things into the glory of heaven.

3 · The Hidden God

Job's complaint has a modern ring (ch. 10): there is little for our subtle philosophers to add to it. God is represented to us in mythical terms as a person whom we might meet; to whom we might appeal; to whose judgement we might submit ourselves; who might pardon us and comfort us. But the person who desires encounters with God finds that this hope is for ever unrealizable. God is the universal life of nations. His hand is everywhere, his face nowhere: the effects of his power can be seen, the purpose of his heart cannot be read. It is senseless to dispute his will, and meaningless to invoke his intervention.

In comment on Job's lament, we may venture a remark on the century-old dispute between theological belief and evolutionary science. We may strike the balance of the debate somewhat as follows. The theologian's strong line is simply to point to the marvels which actually result, where they do result, from the evolutionary process; and then to point to the humbleness of the origins from which they must be supposed to spring, in the bare elements of the world. How can things like the amoeba, not to say physical molecules, have it in them to become you and me? The process of development must have been guided. The conclusion is, first: you cannot have a more persuasive argument for the assisting of natural forces by divine wisdom.

But at the next move, the advantage seems to go over to the sceptical scientist. This happens when we say: God assists natural forces to produce transcendental results. Very well; but in that case we should be able to see just what the forces, left to themselves, would have done, and how the touches of God's hand have moulded and directed them; in a word, what God's assistance has added to the action of nature's elements. But in fact we never can see this. Everything that happens, happens as though through the natural working of natural forces. God's hand is completely hidden: all explanations are natural, not theological, explanations.

Perhaps a simple comparison may be of use here. We hear a conversation on the wireless. The pattern is so right, and the conclusion is so subtly brought about, that we are convinced that some single and highly gifted mind has composed the whole. And yet – let us say – the persons taking part are known to us; and none of them says a word which that person left to himself might not (we feel) perfectly well have said in such a conversation, and on the spur of the moment. What are we to conclude? Perhaps that there was an author to the piece, but that he so well understood the speakers he was writing for, that he made each say what he was himself capable of saying. So the author is completely hidden: his distinct influence cannot be seen in the detail, but merely in the accomplishment of the result.

So God is hidden in his works. He does not shape the forces of action, as a modeller shapes clay: he has so made them that they make the world by acting their natural parts. And so we, like Job, cannot find God in the process, but only and always in the actions of his creatures. His hand is everywhere; his heart, his countenance, his eyes are nowhere; and the person who, like Job, is broken by the process of the world, does not know which way to look for enlightenment or for comfort.

But if this is how God works the world — by making all its components play their natural parts — then how shall he lay bare his heart to us, or reveal the ultimate purpose of his thought-baffling work? How else than through one of his creatures? Everything Jesus does is human and natural, and the speech or act of a Galilean carpenter; and yet through a perfect human nature the God of nature speaks. Where Job was baffled, Philip is enlightened: 'Have I been so long a time with you, and hast thou not known me, Philip? He that has seen me has seen the Father' (John 14.9); and to that Father himself, the root and spring of his being and of his action, Jesus says: 'I have glorified thee on the earth, having accomplished the work thou gavest me to do... I have manifested thy name unto those whom thou gavest me out of the world' (John 17.4,6).

4 · The Holy Name

When the Jews built again the temple Nebuchadnezzar had destroyed, they dared not replace the Ark of the Covenant; the shrine remained empty. It did not too much grieve them that there should be no physical token of God's presence; for had not he said, 'My Name shall be there'? It is difficult for you and me to imagine how they thought, or to conceive that a temple of stone should be built to house a name. Surely the only proper temple for God's Name is a human heart. That God is present to our thoughts by his Name, is no mystery, since it is by their names that our friends find lodgement there. It is round our friends' remembered names that the care we have for them and the pleasure we take in them twine themselves and find a permanent focus. So God is present to us by his Name, and by that presence makes our heart his temple. When we speak to him we address ourselves to his Name within us; and God, being Spirit and universal power, actually moves us and touches us and makes himself felt through his Name which dwells in us.

Nothing can be more sacred to us, more to be had in

reverence and love than this holy Name with which our heart converses; and so the Collect for today is a prayer for fear and affection towards the Name of God. The original Latin is even clearer. It runs thus:

> Make thy Holy Name, O Lord, to be held by us continually in equal reverence and love: forasmuch as thou leavest not unblessed by thy protection those whom thou trainest up to constancy in thine affection: through Jesus Christ our Lord.

5 · The Friendship of Jesus

They used to tell me that our holy religion is a friendship with the Son of God and I wondered what on earth they meant. They gave me Thomas à Kempis to read, and I found a chapter headed 'On personal friendship with Jesus Christ'. 'This man', I said, 'has private conversations with our Lord who is in heaven, but I do not have these conversations and I do not know what it would be like for me to have them. I think my hair would stand on end.' I went out, and I found some people who said: 'Believe the Creed and receive the sacrament and keep the commandments. That is union with the Son of God.' 'Good,' said I, 'I can understand that.'

But now it seems to me that the first people were in a manner right, though they did not explain themselves well; and that was a pity, because everything that Jesus Christ did in this world was, if you look at it, a setting forth of that mysterious divine friendship into which he has taken us, and in order to understand it we do not have to make up any explanations: we just have to attend to him, and see what he does.

11

I will begin by giving you a set of words: Jesus Christ is always uniting himself with us by separating himself from us. As a mere set of words it is nonsense, isn't it, 'union by separation'. Still, if you will just hold the words for the present, I will try to supply the sense in giving you the story. Take the relations of Jesus with his mother: I think they are specially revealing. He began by identifying himself with her completely: well, he was part of her, was he not? He grew from her; she carried him about in herself. That was the starting point. Yet he was so one with her, so confused with her, that she could not get at him, had little joy of him except by anticipation. He separated himself from her by physical birth, and gave her a better union with him by the very fact of such a separation. Now she could handle him; now she could look into his eyes: he was more hers than ever. Yet an infant is but a living doll: he is too much yours for true possession. You do everything for him, put yourself upon him, you get out of him much what you put in.

Jesus separated himself again; he stayed behind in the temple at Jerusalem, and Mary sought him sorrowing. Now he had separated his mind from her, as well as his body: he was thinking his own thoughts, and declaring his own loyalty to a mysterious heavenly parent in that parent's house. He was separated, but Mary's union with him was enriched by the separation. For, we read, he came down to Nazareth with her and submitted himself to her. For now he had a self to submit; it was not now just a biddable child, this boy who put aside his own plans to serve his mother's commands. It is better, she might think, now he gives himself to me, having a self to give and the will to give it.

Another separation: Jesus left his mother's house and went on his mission, and we read how Mary grieved, good woman, because he neglected to feed himself, and came to fetch him to his dinner at an inopportune moment. He would not come, he set her aside for his work. She grieved, no doubt; but do not you think she came more to value through that very separation a son enriched with so divine a work? Once he had been hers, now she was proud to be called his, and found her happiness in the bond with a son whose works and words were full of godhead. Her love was an entering into his life by prayer and sympathy and active aid; sharing him with others, she was none the poorer.

He separated himself again – but this is not the time to think of the separation of the cross, so speedily recovered in the resurrection. Her son lived, and shared himself alive – he might even be touched, so we read, that dear flesh which she had borne in her womb. Yet he would not remain – there was a last separation, he ascended, and what, you will think, could Mary do but weep? But this separation merely continued the line of the others, and enriched the union. For if it had been a nobler thing for Mary's heart to go along with Jesus in his earthly mission than to have him in her lap, it was a nobler thing for her to go along with him in his heavenly reign than to follow his earthly steps. The Jesus with whom she now unites herself is in the whole living Church and in the whole operation of the love of God. He is in the least of his brethren – in John, for instance, whom Jesus gave to Mary from the cross, both instead of himself and as a part of himself. 'Woman, behold thy son' has a double sense.

Follow Jesus from the womb of Mary to his heavenly throne and you will see in what manner he has made friends with us and what sort of a friendship he has made. He gives us a portion of his mind, lifts us into union with his purposes, shows us himself: his wounds in the unfortunate and his eyes in the saints. And as we dwell with affection on our friends' names and taste the very flavour of them on our tongues, so the most commonplace of Christians pronounces the name of Jesus with the warmth of recognition, tasting and seeing that the Lord is gracious. It is a good prayer, simply the name of Jesus said as it should be said: it tells us what we are, and what our friends are, and what our God is, and what he has done for us and for our salvation.

6 · A Father's Love

Your words have been strong against me, says the voice of
the Lord, pleading with his people for their love (Mal.
3.13). Wherein have we spoken against thee? they reply,
for none of us admit what is the truth, that we hate God's
will and complain of his ways with a great part of our
minds, for a great part of the time. Wherein have we
spoken against God? In thinking like this: can it really
make all the difference, that we serve God, when people
around us do not, and are apparently happy? Is our
abstinence better than their indulgence? You have said (so
the divine voice continues) it is vain to serve God; and what
profit is it that we have kept his charge and that we have
walked mournfully before the Lord of Hosts? And now we
call the proud happy — yes, the proud, above all, the
proud: how we envy those who devote themselves to
building themselves up, and putting themselves across,
and who get away with it! They live unscrupulously and
(says the prophet) they are built up: they tempt God, they
ask for trouble; and they are delivered, they pull it off. . . .

After this fashion they that fear the Lord speak one with

15

another, and the Lord hearkeneth and heareth (which is very much more than they deserve) and a book of remembrance is written before him for them that fear the Lord and that think upon his name: a book where he sees their names always before him, as your friends' names are, perhaps, always before you in your notebook of intercessions, if, that is, you remember to look into it, or if, indeed, you have remembered in the first place to write them there. They shall be mine, saith the Lord, those whose names are written; in the great day of reckoning that I make, they shall be to me a peculiar treasure; their names have been ever in my heart, their lives shall be in my hands. And I will spare them as a man spareth his own son that serveth him. Then you shall turn and perceive the difference between the righteous and the wicked, between him that serveth God and him that serveth him not.

Yes, said the righteous son who served his father, I think I can perceive the difference. For now that I have served my father all day in the field, laboriously, I shall return, and there will be my place by the fire; there is the kind old man who depends on me more and more and whose place I shall inherit, when that fool my young brother has run through the portion he took out in cash, and begs from door to door. There is certainly a difference. But what is this on in the house? Music and dancing. What's that you say? My father has slain the fatted calf? Why, he never gave me a kid to make merry with my friends. It makes no kind of difference to him: he simply doesn't care.

But his father came out and embraced him. Son, thou art ever with me, and all that is mine is thine. But it was meet to make merry and be glad, for this thy brother was dead and is alive again, was lost, and is found. And do not talk to me of what you read there in the page of the prophets. They shall return and see the difference between him that serveth and him that serveth not, for you have not read to the end of the matter. 'Lo, I will send you Elijah the prophet before the great and terrible day of the Lord comes. And he shall turn the heart of the father to the children, and the heart of the child to the father, lest at my coming I smite the earth with a curse' (Mal. 4.5–6). Elijah has performed his task, and pointed to the Son, in whose obedience all my rebellious children are reconciled; who served for the wages of rejection and was obedient not unto life but to the death; who was himself slain to furnish the feast, at which repentant prodigals shall dance and sing.

7 · Holy Fire

In St Paul's First Epistle to the Corinthians (ch. 14), the Apostle tells us how, in the early days of the Church, a person would be seized with ecstasy and pour out the praises of God in sounds that were not even articulate. It was difficult to know what to do about this, for on the one hand it seemed impious to check the motions of the Spirit, but on the other hand, the believers would not be much edified by listening to meaningless utterances, however fervid. St Paul's advice is that those seized with ecstasy should seek solitude, and have their outpouring of heart between themselves and God: for God, he says, knows what the Spirit within us is crying, even when we do not know ourselves. There is one exception, however, to the Apostle's advice in favour of solitude for ecstatics. Sometimes, he says, the same Spirit which gives the ecstasy interprets the sense of it: either the ecstatic himself, or one of those sitting by, is moved to expound what the mind of the Spirit is. In such a case there is no need for the ecstatic to seek solitude: he can edify the Church through an interpreter.

What had happened then on the first Christian Pentecost? The Apostles, who had never experienced ecstasy and knew nothing about it, were suddenly seized with a great glory, like fire, like a gale of the breath of God, and burst into the strange sort of speech. On this occasion there was no need of an interpreter; for God himself interpreted the message direct to the hearts of the motley crowd of pilgrims who collected there. It came home to each of them with the intimacy of his mother-tongue – but not to all: some, who lacked the illumination, thought the Apostles were drunk. You will notice that St Luke does not exaggerate the miracle. The message conveyed to the hearers was something quite general, which they could reasonably have gathered from religious ecstasy – they knew that the wonderful works of God were being praised. That was all. They did not understand the Christian gospel until St Peter, returning to a normal state of consciousness, began to preach to them.

These things happened, said St Luke, when the Day of Pentecost was fully come: as though the old Jewish feast would provide some sort of impetus for the occurrence he describes. And so, indeed, it would. What did the pious Jew think about on the Day of Pentecost? What (consequently) were St Peter and his friends thinking about that day, when the ecstasy seized them? About the great voice which had poured from the lips of God in fire from the top of Sinai, and given Israel the law. The divine voice, the rabbis taught, spoke from the mountain top in the languages of all the nations on earth, but only Israel's ear was tuned to hear. As they thought on these things the Apostles were seized: the voice of ecstasy, a voice they could not control, not theirs but as it were the voice of God, poured forth; but this time it came home to the ears and hearts of all nations, gathered in Jerusalem to keep the feast of Pentecost. God speaks no longer from the

19

mountain top, he speaks through human lips. His law is not for twelve tribes now, it is for all the nations of the earth. Nor is it written on tablets of stone and set before their eyes: it is written by the finger of God on the tablets of their hearts; written in the letters of love and desire. For this is the supreme miracle of inspiration: God makes us love his holy will and delight in it, because it is glorious and clean and joyful, and our everlasting good.

8 · All Saints

I will tell you a Jewish story from the time soon after
Christ. Some pagans were teasing a couple of little Jewish
girls, and trying to laugh them out of their religion. What
could be more absurd than the hope of resurrection? How
shall the person rotted and gone to clay ever live and
breathe again? The little Jewesses whispered together for a
moment. Then one of them said: 'May I tell you a story,
please?' 'Go on', said the others. 'In our village,' said she,
'there were two potters. One of them could make pots out
of water and clay. The other could make pots out of water
alone. Which of them, do you think, was the more
surprising in his skill?' 'Well, of course, you are talking
nonsense,' they said, 'but if there were such men, the
making of pots out of mere water would be much more
surprising.' 'Then why are you more surprised', said the
child, 'that God should make new again out of clay, than
that he should have made them out of a drop of water in the
beginning?'

I don't think there is much to be added by the wisest
head to this childish argument. If we believe in God at all,

we believe in the creator through whose will and power all things, including human beings, have come to be, not from a drop of water, but from nothing. If he makes us again, at least he has some materials; even though the way he works on them is an absolute mystery to us. Nevertheless, it would be a strange sort of belief which allowed God to have had the power to create all things, and yet denied him the power to remake the human person.

The commemoration of All Saints is not concerned with those who lived particularly holy lives on earth, but with those whom the power of God has remade and brought through to heaven. To believe in the real existence of this great company is not to believe in something called the soul, which cannot die: it is to believe in God, and in his will to save us alive and bring us near himself. The saints have been made by God in their creation, and remade by him in their heavenly existence. But more, they have been made what they are by heavenly grace. God has not only given them existence, he has given them sanctity; and that is why we have fellowship with them, and are bound in one communion of saints. For the divine love which has triumphed in them will also conquer us. If we want to know what God is doing with us, we look at these splendid beings who share the spontaneity of the creator's mind, the delight of his heart and the breath of his love. Religion is not fundamentally a battle against sin, it is a drawing up together into glorification. God draws us above all through Jesus Christ, and Christ through all those who have gone before us, or who accompany us. Not all those, we think, who have left this earthly scene have yet reached that heavenly one, and so, as we rejoice in all saints today, we pray for all souls tomorrow, especially for the friends we knew, that God will join them to the saints, through Jesus Christ.

9 · God's Will and Mine

Our independent freedom of will is very slight: it is the conscious surface of the mind; but then, what depths beneath, of which we have little notion, and which, doubtless, affect our actions to an indeterminable extent. When I still used to try to swim, I felt very brave if I crossed deep water; but I was careful not to think of the terrible way down it was between my feet and the bottom; I concentrated on the surface, and tried to be cheerful. And so, no doubt, it is with our conscious life. We keep to the surface of our mind and think we are free. We make a great to-do with our kicking and striking, and think that we are going where we choose; but when we look round and take our bearings, we find it is the currents that have carried us.

The good swimmer who is a stranger to the stretch of shore will be drowned for all his swimming: he cannot make out against the tide. But familiarity with the water will save even the moderate swimmer: he will know about the back currents, and will strike into them. The tide will go out, but he will come in, swept on the curve of the shoreward water.

Well, we must swim, for else we shall drown – I mean, we must exercise our will. Unremitting endeavour, that has been the way of the saints. And yet, by our will alone, how little we can do. For we must love, that is the first command: we must love God, and our neighbour too, with a Godlike care: if we cannot love, we achieve nothing: no, not though we speak with the tongues of angels, not though we master all the mysteries of knowledge, or even (it would tax our virtue to the limit) even though we give away all we have and put on the Franciscan robe. We get nowhere, unless we love; but is love at command? Can I do it by setting my jaw and clenching my hands? Stiffen the sinews, summon up the blood, imitate the action of the tiger? No: heaven save us from tigerish Christians, stalking about like the devil himself, seeking whom they may devour.

I am commanded to love, and love is not at command; and yet I know where the currents of charity run, and I can strike into them. Ezekiel saw a vision (ch. 47): a great head of water, clear, abundant and sweet, broke from under the sill of the temple, on the high droughty hills. East and west it rolled in a flood: eastwards down to the Dead Sea, and everywhere the water went, life arose. The currents of sweet water spread through the brackish lake, and everywhere they went, fishes began to swarm. And such are we: such are our souls, alive only in those sweet currents that spread this way and that from the first Pentecost, healing the brackish sea. And can we find our way into these currents? Yes: we can go into our chamber, and shut the door, and pray to our Father who hears in secret, in union of mind with the Redeemer who gave us this command; and we can wait for his Spirit. We will name God, and God himself will give the love that carries us to meet him; we will name our friends, and our enemies too, if we have any, and God's care for them will move us. God is our freedom, God is our power: for God is Spirit.

10 · The Voice of God

Isaiah's message (30.15–18) is so terrifyingly applicable to our situation, one is afraid to touch it. What was happening? His countrymen felt the pride of a great spiritual heritage, a pride which contrasted strangely with the weakness of their political position: they were no longer a first-class power, they were threatened by a mammoth empire from the east (to be precise, the north-east), and saw their only hope in the support of an apparently equal power lying to their west (or to be exact their south-west). They tried to hold together a sort of NATO system of Western Asiatic States, and it looked all right until it was tested, but then it went down like cardboard. Cavalry, as you will observe, was the arm they relied on in those days. So many horses were terribly expensive to keep up, but, as the prophet remarks, they would be splendid to run away upon. God, he says, has called Israel to quietness and confidence, a policy of non-provocation; but no, they would gamble on an all-or-nothing result. And such was their excitement, so utterly were they bound up in the politics of power, that God could do nothing with them.

But, says the prophet, God is patient. He will wait until their disease has run its course, and their fever has burnt itself out in the smouldering ruins of their cities. Then he will arise and have mercy on them. The bread won't be much in those days, and the water will be in short supply, but the voice of the Lord will sound again in their ears, his eyes will meet their eyes, and they will know what to do, how to live.

I am no prophet, nor am I a prophet's son, and I am not going to say (for I do not know) how like or how different our situation is from Israel's in the sight of eternal providence. But I am sure that we do not have to wait, as Israel did, for any storm to gather and break, before we can hear and see God. He taught Israel by the series of events which led to Christ at last, but after that our teacher was to be removed no more, his voice would still be in our ears.

The voice is there, but we cannot hear it any more than Israel could, so long as we are possessed by worldly hope and fear, and staking our hearts on any earthly event. Political anxiety is only one sort of anxiety. It is absurd how, even in a quiet life, we fool ourselves and mismanage ourselves into living from one petty crisis to another. To hear the voice of God we must exorcize our demons. It is often necessary, when we come before him in our prayer, to make a clean breast of our anxieties, just as we do our sins. Perhaps there is going to be a war next year. Well, perhaps there is. Perhaps the girl won't have me. No, perhaps she won't. Perhaps I shall not fool the examiners into giving me a better class in my degree than I deserve. Very likely not. Well now, am I willing to serve you, my God, whatever happens, and to trust you with the event? For this is life eternal, that I should know you, the only true God, through him whom you sent, Jesus Christ. Without waiting for any worldly assurances, he glorified you on the earth, he accomplished the work you gave him to do. He perished on the cross, and you glorified him with your own self with the glory he had before the world was.

11 · Heart to Heart

When modern Christians read ancient Scriptures, they find the action of the Holy Spirit identified with special phenomena of the mind, or even of the body: through divine seizure Elijah suddenly felt his strength doubled, and ran before Ahab's chariot from Carmel to Jezreel; the Spirit came as ecstasy on the companions of Samuel; they danced and raved in honour of their God from morn till night. But in the same way we find the action of God identified with special phenomena of nature: with the wind, for example, which pushed the water back and bared the treacherous sands, when Israel escaped and Pharaoh's chariots foundered. If natural science can give an account of the Red Sea wind, so it can, perhaps, of the prophetic ecstasy. God is not literally to be identified with any physical, or any psychic, force: he is the cause behind causes, his will underlies the very existence of these energies which operate in their own manner; and so the life of the Holy Spirit underlies the action of the sanctified will.

How mysterious a thing, even when science has finished

with it, the action of our will remains! What are the elements that go to make the concentration of purpose, out of which great and effective resolves arise? People often devote their lives to one thing – for example, if it is not indecent to take a living case, we met last term a man who has given himself to save lonely and troubled people from despair and death, and who has done miracles, and earned the blessings of thousands. How did it happen? For nothing would have been accomplished by the mere decision to tidy up a social mess and plug a hole in the welfare services. No: there was contact with unhappiness, the response of the heart, a slow growth of conviction that nothing was worth doing if this task remained undone, the knowledge of a personal call to undertake it, the renunciation of alternative aims. One cannot *make* such a decision about the use of one's life, and yet one has to make it: it is a personal decision, if anything is, and yet it comes together so mysteriously, out of so many elements deep in the mind – and deeper, that is our faith: deeper than the mind, deeper than the very root of the soul is the life of God, the Holy Spirit, on whose inspiration we draw. God calls us from without – he stands beside us in the human form, Jesus Christ. God answers from within: deep answers deep, God answers God. When we pray, we set before our face the God to whom we pray, in the faith that God himself inspires the prayer. How to pray as we should, we have not the skill. But the Spirit himself intercedes for us in sighs that lack articulate expression; while the Searcher of hearts knows the meaning of the Spirit; for in praying on behalf of God's servants, he prays the will of God.

12 · Moving God's Heart

The cool and rational eye of the anthropologist is turned on the religious practices of the human race: he studies the ceremonies and sacrifices of human tribes as a naturalist studies the social pattern of the ant-hill or the beehive. Viewing them as though from a great height, he sees his little men dance round and round their smoking altars, and asks himself what they are doing. Not, evidently, what they say. For they say that their circular dance is danced for putting strength into the sun, that he may not flag in the successive laps of his unending race, nor lack the vigour to prevail over the mist, but, dispersing it in due time, may ripen their corn. This is what they say, but it cannot be what they do: for dance as they may, they cannot dance the sun round the sky. What do they really do? They cannot put heart into the sun, but they can hearten themselves. Faced with the desolating uncertainty of the seasons, they encourage themselves to plough, and sow, and weed, by weaving a magic bond of sympathy between themselves and the luminary who is the master of their hopes.

The anthropologist may be a Christian, and even, as Fr

Schmidt was, a Christian priest. The mass bell rings: he shuts up the book he is reading, with its eye-witness accounts of curious Polynesian rites; he shuts the book, he vests and goes into the church; he and his server begin to move about the altar with measured steps in a beloved and traditional pattern; he turns his face, and lifts his hands upward; he prays for sunshine and for rain. He whose visionary eye was but now fixed from a height of great detachment on the ritual acts of others, comes himself under the scrutiny of a thousand eyes, and, wondered at by men and angels, offers the Christian sacrifice for sun and rain. Shall he exempt himself from the critique of his own science? Will his hands move the sun, will his incantation shake the clouds? How is he better than those benighted heathen, whose childish ways awaken his grave compassion? Religion has not suddenly become a different thing: as I move about the altar, as I break and give the bread, I am still dancing myself and you into sympathy with the heart behind the world. I cannot hope to do any better at moving the world than the heathen do, for I too am a human being. But God has done better, there's the difference: he has done better things for me, for he has disclosed to me the heart which is the heart of the world; and specially on that day, and in that place, when it was laid open to us by the blade of a soldier's spear, and there came out water and blood. Then the veil of the temple was rent from the top to the bottom, the sky cracked and rolled up, and God came through.

The prayer of superstition hopes to put into God the heart to love us: we cannot put heart into God, it is he who puts heart into us, his own heart.

Not above the thunder cloud, not behind sun or moon, beats the heart in rhythm with which my prayer must move: no, God has buried it here, right under the root of my will. I will go through the motions, I will speak the words, but God will give the Spirit. And in the Spirit the Church shall pray: she shall ask for sun and rain, for plenty and for peace, for everything it is wholesome and natural we should desire, that our wishes for these things, and the undertakings our wishes prompt, may be prayed into harmony with almighty love, through the Spirit that lurks in us.

13 · The Narrow Gulf

The world spreads round me in circles. The first circle is feeling, which reaches as far as the boundaries of my body. The second circle is sight, which slides out along the lines of light as far as sun, moon and stars. The third circle is thought, which, building on the evidence of instruments, extends into a world of stars beyond the stars I see. My knowledge fans outwards from my body to the bodies which make my environment, and so out and out to bodies beyond these, until my environment includes the universe of stars. My habit is to plot the position of everything I take for real somewhere in the unending field of bodies. If I said of something that it was outside the bodily field I could only mean that it was in the outer part of it, beyond any bodies my thought had previously reached.

Where, then, in all my spreading world is Jesus Christ, the man risen and glorified? When clouds received him from our sight, into what height, what distance did he go? However far away I place him, I gain nothing by it: he fits no better beyond Orion than behind the nearest trees. His risen being is no part of our interlocked system of bodily force, whether far or near. He is nowhere in this world. He is not outside it, either, for it hasn't got an outside where he could be. Where is he, then?

It is useless to start from me, and to fan out and out, looking for Jesus Christ: I must start from Jesus Christ, and fan out from there until I reach myself. Jesus is the heart and centre of heaven, just as each of us is the heart and centre of our own world. He is assured of his own world as each of us is assured of ours – through his own living existence: he knows he is there, and as the action of his life is more intense and wakeful than ours, he has less temptation than the best employed of us ever to take existence from a dream. His life is even less locked than ours is within his own breast. Radiating through lines of heavenly sympathy, his soul knows what is next to him, blessed saints whose society forms the very place of his existence; and so out and out, without failure or weakening of sight, his eyes embrace a universe of spirits, as many as the stars we see. Without thinning or flattening of sound he may converse with the distant as with the near, and receive back voices in answer to his voice, expressing each in its unique and personal colour the glory and the love of God.

At first it may seem that we have two answers, spreading on independent planes and nowhere touching at a single point. Christ's universe of spirit, and ours of physical force. Yet thinking further we perceive that it cannot be so. For while it is indeed impossible to place heaven in the world, it is impossible not to place the world in heaven. If Christ's knowledge is spiritual, as ours is physical, then he knows us, for we are spirits too, spirits in fleshly bodies; and if he knows our spirits, he knows what our spirits know, including their bodily knowledge. He hears us speak from within our throats; he thinks our thoughts as fast as we can form them. But he feels in our fingers too, and looks through our eyes; he lives out along the lines of our vision, and our sun, moon and stars are his. By sheer love, heaven grafts the world into itself, and roots our universe in its own heart.

Jesus Christ, living Son of the living God, clothed in our nature, I cannot place you in my world, but neither can I escape from yours. I cannot reach you by many steps, but I can reach you by one, the single step of faith which lands me in the heart of heaven. If ever I am to end with you, it is from you I must begin. Thou God seest me; and if ever I am to see across the gulf from me to you, it will be by starting with you, and seeing myself through your holy and compassionate eyes.

14 · Judgement and Mercy

Some of us were sitting the other evening, talking about our religion and running our heads once more against the impenetrable difficulty of divine justice and how we are to reconcile it with infinite and inexhaustible mercy. There we sat, and we were really speculating, I suppose, on what we should do if we were sitting, not in the ground floor of the college quadrangle, but on the Throne of the Universe. Now I do not say that it is wrong for us to place ourselves in imagination on the Throne of Majesty: but I do record the fact that whenever we do place ourselves there our thought dies in us. We have the sensation of playing an empty charade. Nothing is real any more. We are told that Moses was summoned into the heart of Glory, and God spoke to him there; but then he was summoned, and God spoke to him. When we of our own will try to walk into the heart of Glory, and fix the central point of all being with our own measuring tape, we find nothing but the centre of emptiness. To find God all we need to do is to return into ourselves; we shall find God in what he does to us. God's throne is an impenetrable darkness, or, if you

35

prefer to say so, a brightness utterly blinding, out of which proceed lightnings, and thunderings and voices. The points of the lightning are thrown just so far as to touch us, the arrowheads of the voices bury themselves in our hearts.

When we read the ancient prophets, Hosea for example, we are not invited to the centre of the mystery, to spy at God, we are placed at the circumference and our breasts are bared to the arrows that fly out of the throne: arrows of judgement, arrows of love. The God behind the darkness, whose thoughts I cannot see, kills and he makes alive. Whether he shoots from the same bow the shafts of ice and the shafts of fire, I do not know, but I know that both are as sharp as death and both are pushed home by omnipotence, and that I must not turn away, but take both in my heart. To expose sin to holiness is to suffer annihilation. According to the good pasture I gave them, says Hosea's God of his rebellious sheep, they gorged themselves and their heart was uplifted; and so they have forgotten me. Therefore am I a lion unto them, as a leopard I watch their way, I meet them as a bear bereaved of her whelps and I rend the caul of their heart. But equally, to the first sign of penitence mercy is unconfined. 'I heal their backsliding, I love them freely; mine anger is turned from them; I am as the dew to Israel, he shall flourish as the lily.' These are the things God does to sin and to repentance; both are immeasurably strong, for both are God; and yet we know that of two immeasurable things, judgement and mercy, mercy prevails.

15 · Letters of Truth

The Book of Daniel is remembered for the gallery of impressive symbolical pictures it presents: the three young Israelites in the burning fiery furnace, Nebuchadnezzar eating grass like an ox, Daniel in the den of lions; and to these we may add, the writing on the wall. The king of great Babylon used to write decrees, or rather, his scribe wrote them down, and his mason cut in imperishable stone the sentence of his lips, that it might stand unchangeably forever. He made gods to be gods by the breath of his mouth, and placed himself among the gods, the more to glorify his throne. He said it, and it was so. But as for the true God, who said and it was so, who said there should be light, and it was so, who said that King Belshazzar should be, and it was so: Belshazzar's father had pulled down his temple at Jersualem, and Belshazzar himself, on a fatal night, sent for the spoils of the temple, the golden bowls of sacrifice that Solomon had made, and drank from them with the women of his harem and the flatterers of his court. Then, says the Jewish moral tale, the hand of the scribe of heaven appeared and wrote a decree on the wall: the truth of God which stood, and there was no gainsaying it. The king turned pale and the sham omnipotence of mighty Babylon melted in the night.

The new masters of the world sent the Jews home and the Temple rose from its ashes. And so it happened on a certain day that there walked across the Temple courts the scribes of Israel, the men who copied out divine dictation, and thought that they could write decrees as firm and solid as the world, and bind them on the necks of men. They dragged with them a caught adulteress, going to her judgement and her penalty. But then as they went, they met Truth standing by a pillar, dressed in the frock of a Galilean workman. 'Master,' they said to Truth, 'Moses told us to stone such: what sayest thou?' Truth stooped and wrote with his finger in the dust; then lifting himself, 'Let he that is sinless among you,' he said, 'be the first to cast a stone.' He stooped and went on writing. What was the finger of Truth writing against them on the pavement? It needed no Daniel, skilled in miracles and omens, to interpret to each man of them the half-seen letters in the dust. Every man was the Daniel of his own heart, and as the writing ran across the pavement, letters of fire came up in the conscience of them all. The woman found herself alone with Truth, and saw his eyes. 'Woman, where are they? Did no one condemn you?' Lord, not one. 'Neither do I condemn you: go and sin no more.'

St John, the ageing apostle of Incarnate Truth, moves his pen over the parchment, tracing a message which is to remain among his spiritual children. Children (this is what forms itself under his pen), let us not love with word or tongue but in deed and in truth. Hereby we shall know we belong to Truth and shall persuade our heart in his sight, whatever condemnation our heart may press on us, that God is greater than our heart, and knoweth all things (1 John 3.18–20). Our heart knows itself – not well, indeed, but in part – and condemns itself. God is greater than our heart, and he knows it well, he knows it through and through, and if we could read God's knowledge of our heart, we should condemn ourselves to worse than stoning. God knows our heart, but God is greater than our heart, and knows, not our heart only, but all things: especially one thing, his own heart. He knows that he has loved us with an everlasting love, and will not let us go.

16 · To the Father's House

The repentance of the Prodigal Son does no one any credit. Christ's stories are never edifying, always realistic. If you found yourself on a wet afternoon so destitute of all means of tolerable occupation as to be reduced to reading a parish magazine, and if you found a serial inset, 'The Prodigal Son', by Millicent Mincing, what would you expect the story to be like? After much anaemic description of riotous living you can bet your life that Miss Mincing will get round to touching the young man's heart: either he is going to encounter misery greater than his own, patiently borne, and turned into a blessing for others; or he is going to be compassionately fed himself by a hand that he has treacherously bitten. In either case he dissolves in weeping or (alternatively) with dry and manly eyes experiences a regret too serious for tears. Lord, he says, how could I do this to you? Dare I hope that you will ever forgive me?

Well: but in the gospel parable there is none of this. Everybody drops the spendthrift like a hot brick as soon as his money is gone. No one edifies him by singing hymns with him over a diet of husks. Someone gives him work, but no one anything you could call pay. It dawns on him that he has not been so clever as he supposed: he could have done better at home. Why, the labourers who work for his father are actually paid every Friday! The young man's stomach is touched, so is his pocket; but the old man is touched to the heart. For the story, as I began by saying, is realistic; and you are no doubt well aware that the happiness of your parents is more bound up in you than yours in them: a fact which may make them interfering, tiresome, exacting, and incline you to beat it for a far country; but which will always make them forgive you your callousness, if you give them half a chance, and incline them to accept perfunctory protestations as signs of filial affection.

Such is life. But Christ did not tell the story so that his hearers might say, Such is life, but that they might say, Such is God, and such are we. There is nothing heroic or edifying about our repentances. The world, when it does not write religion off as nonsense, thinks of it as a high-minded and creditable pursuit which we are sometimes noble enough to spare time for. But no, says Christ's parable, our devout and God-fearing times are merely those in which we recover our minds from a spendthrift folly: when we see that bread and cheese are better than pigwash; that to live by the will of God is our natural happiness, our sunlight, our warmth, our food, our drink, our breathable air. While as for God, his heart towards us is the heart of a parent: he is eager to reward, and over-reward, a mere surrender to his will. We give him some half-sentences, and the tenth part of our heart (we cannot give the rest if we try) and he gives us the bread of heaven. Herein is love, says St John's Epistle, not that we love God, but that he has loved us, and given his Son to be the expiation of our sins.

17 · God our Maker

The prophets of Israel were not much like academic philosophers and they never attempted to be fair to their opponents. Their account of contemporary idolatry was an outrageous caricature. It was quite untrue that, while Israel worshipped a transcendent spirit, her heathen neighbour worshipped carved and painted images, supposing them to be gods. The heathen knew very well that deity is spirit and that an image is at the most a means whereby the god is pleased to make himself present or known. Would Isaiah have been impressed by such a defence? I do not think so. 'If what you say is true,' he would have replied, 'why don't you stop making idols?' The error is practical, not theoretical. God is above the world, and distinct from any representation of him. Agreed. But if so, without tokens or representations of him, how is he to be known or invoked? There are only two possibilities. Either we shall find God in what we do or make: and that is idolatry. Or we shall acknowledge God in what he makes or does: and that is true religion. The God of Israel is neither a myth of the poets nor a sculpture of the statuaries. He is a power known in his deeds: the hand that delivered us from Egypt, the heart that bore with our rebellions, the word that speaks in the mouth of his prophets, the Spirit which moves us to face death to the death.

Either in what he makes, or in what we make. If that is the choice, then, as you can see, literal and physical idolatry is only the extreme case of a much wider aberration. There is a religious exercise rightly recommended to us all, and that is meditation: reflective Bible-reading is the best-known form of it. You read your Scripture, and you think about it: you think who (on this evidence) God is, and what he can be trusted to do. You have certainly begun in the right place, not with any man-made idol, but (let us say) with the record of Christ's acts or words. Yet the picture you form, and the expectation you find, will be what you make; and if you worship this as God, you may be moving towards idolatry. But what alternative is there? You must do the thinking, yes. But then you throw yourself on God. You say to God: Don't let me make you; here I am, make me; I shall know you in the making. You have given me tokens of the way you deal with your servants, but it is not for me to hold you to your words: you are the master. What you do will be like you, and divinely right, but it lies in your wisdom, not in my imagination, to say what it shall be.

We make idols of our friends, not only of God; but there the error is less desperate. For we have more ability to see what our friends are, so that the image has more truth. And in some degree, we can actually create our friends by our imaginative constructions; for people always, to some extent, accept our estimate of them and act the part we devise for them. It may happen sometimes, and indeed often, that we do them no harm by so forming or shaping them; for it may well be that what we expect of them is better than what they would otherwise be; and the same will be true about their expectations of us. Christians love one another into being better people. Nevertheless, too much of this is stifling; we must let people be what they are. And how much more, God! He is what he is: this is the Name by which he will be known, I am what I am. That is why there is no worship we can offer, other than faith and obedience.

18 · Who can Forgive?

The Pharisees protested that God alone could forgive sins: and the Pharisees were right (Mark 2.1–12). Sins are offences against God, and none but the offended person can give away his right to satisfaction. If boys come and steal my fruit, and you go and tell them that no one minds in the least, you will certainly be acting *ultra vires*; and if I catch the young thieves, I will punish them just the same. But then I might have given you the job of finding the little culprits, and put it at your discretion what to do with them. If you are satisfied that you have frightened them sufficiently, and that they won't repeat the crime, you may let them off with a caution; if not, denounce them to the police, and I promise that what you do, I will support. Now the Pharisees knew that God had, under various covenants and by various acts of inspiration, empowered various men to act in his name: Aaron to take away pollutions, David to rule his chosen people, Elijah to pronounce his judgements. But, the Pharisees said, and quite correctly too, God had never given men the power in his name to absolve sins committed against his person. The

Israelite sinner was simply left to hope in the mercies of his God. But now Jesus shows them a new thing. Man *has* been entrusted with the power to forgive sins: not, of course, *any* man, but the man perfect, the man absolute, the man in whom that divine likeness we all remotely share becomes a portrait painted to the life: the Son of Man, that glorious figure whom Daniel's vision had foretold — he has been empowered to forgive sins. How can so astounding a claim be proved? Anyone might try to get away with the claim to have forgiven someone's sins; no visible devils would fly from the forgiven sinner's nostrils, to show that his sins were banished from his heart. No, but not anyone could get away with saying to the sinner — he happens also to be a paralytic — 'Arise and walk': for either the man would walk, or he would not. And such was the sign that Jesus gave. It was, for the moment, the only sign he could give; it was not the final sign, nor the adequate sign. For, though it is harder to get away with 'Arise and walk' than it is to get away with 'Thy sins are forgiven thee', still, it is a greater thing to forgive sins than to heal paralysis; and not every practitioner who has the healing touch can forgive sins against God. Still, for the while, Christ gave them this sign; it was all he could do: he raised the paralytic, who to all appearances was as dead as a stick. But the true and adequate sign he gave when the Pharisees, unconvinced by all his signs, unconverted by a sinless life, or by a radiance of grace, nailed him to the cross and brought him to the sepulchre: wrapped, embalmed, as dead as a stick. But then he rose, in power and glory, to press God's forgiveness on those who had killed him, and for whom, as the nails went in, he had prayed.

Peter and John, entering into the Temple soon after the resurrection of Jesus, found a paralytic beggar lying at the gate (Acts 3). Him, in the Name of Christ whose commission they bore, the two apostles raised up, and standing

with him there, they preached to the astonished neigh-
bours the raising up of Jesus and the forgiveness of sins.
'Ye killed the Prince of Life,' said Peter, 'whom God raised
up from the dead.... Repent, therefore, and turn again,
that your sins may be blotted out, and that there come
seasons of refreshing from the presence of the Lord....
Since to you first God, having raised his servant up, hath
sent him to bless you, in turning every one of you from
your iniquities.' So, then, this free pardon, proclaimed by
Christ, is the great boon offered to us continually, and to be
embraced by us upon our knees every day when we acknowledge that we have not worthily borne before the
world that Holy Name which our Christian profession has
stamped upon our foreheads. Our paralysis is in the will:
and this shall heal it.

19 · God's Caring

The fable of Jonah is profoundly ironical. The climax of irony is the point at which the prophet complains that his God is sure to let him down, because he is faithful to the character in which he had revealed himself to Moses. When Moses asked to see the face of God, it was denied him; but, says the sacred legend, God put him in a cleft of the rock and covered it with his hand, while majesty swept by, and the air quivered with a voice which makes and unmakes the world. Thus God proclaimed himself: 'The Lord, the Lord, a God full of compassion and gracious, slow to anger, and plenteous in mercy and truth, keeping mercy for thousands, forgiving iniquity and sin.' There you are, says Jonah, that's you all over; so what is the use of carrying your messages of impending wrath? You are sure to take pity and call off the lightning; and then a pretty fool your messenger looks: thirty days, and Nineveh is *not* overthrown. This is, perhaps, the high water mark of irony; but the divine speech with which the story ends is still deeply ironical. If Jonah had pity on the gourd, which came up in a day and perished in a day, should not God have pity on Nineveh? You will protest that Jonah did not have pity on the gourd, his pity was all for himself. Of course that is the irony. Perhaps we should get the point better if we found an English phrase which disguises the sarcasm a little more effectively. You were sorry about the gourd: and should not I be sorry about the Ninevites . . . ? If your selfish regret is natural to you, I call on you to recognize that unselfish regret is natural to me. If God regretted the gourd, it would be for its own sake. A gourd is not much, but it is beautiful and vital, it contains several million parts, intricately organized. A hackneyed line tells of human regret:

> Men are we, and must grieve when even the shade
> Of that which once was great has passed away.

What similar or contrasting words would we dare to place on divine lips?

> God am I, and must grieve when even the least
> Of things ephemeral has had its day.

Jonah's selfish report about the gourd is no more than a parody of God's dispassionate care: and God's care for plants, that today flourish and tomorrow go into the oven, is nothing compared with his care for the Ninevites. He sees the sparrow fall; he sees a life, a light more precious than a star extinguished; and turns his eyes to the fledglings nurtured to take its place. He cannot be comforted so, for those who are made in his own image and likeness, unless he can rescue them each one, and save them everlastingly.

Jonah is called upon to see the Ninevites through the eyes of God: not as people whose fate will make Jonah his prophetic reputation, but as beings who are the objects of everlasting pity. St Paul (in Philippians 4) calls on his friends to share God's pure concern for things as they

49

are, seen in their own proper values. 'Whatsoever things are true, whatsoever things are to be revered, whatsoever things are just, whatsoever things are pure, whatsoever things are lovely, whatsoever things are gracious; if there be any virtue, if there be any merit, have an eye for these things.' How damnable is the religion which narrows our sympathy and prejudices our judgements, and prevents us from seeing the beauty and the pitiableness of things as they are! Christians should pray with the heart of God, especially when they offer their intercession for his creatures.

20 · Coats from God

It has been said that the story of the fall in the Garden of
Eden is a drama out of which the divine Actor emerges
with little credit; but you must reflect on two points: first,
that the devil is a liar, and, second, that Genesis does not
contain the end of the story. The devil is a liar: we must
not accept his account of the matter as true. He is a liar
when he says that disobedience, the throwing off of the
loving yoke of God's will, is going to make us gods on our
own account, able to assess the good and evil of things by
reference to ourselves alone, and without reference to their
place in the divine purposes. Our acceptance of the
serpent's account when we read the story is an instinctive
act of sympathy on our part — we are so used to believing
the forked tongue which hisses in our own ears, that we
naturally believe it when we read what it hissed in the ears
of Eve. God is our full, our sole and our everlasting good:
having God walking with us in the cool of the day, when
we pray, and in the heat of the day too, when we labour —
that is life, that is illumination; that is what opens the eyes,
for with God in our heart we see what we are, and what

51

other people are, and what the glories of nature, this universal Eden, are; rebellion against God casts a shadow and darkness on all our ways, and on all his works. God is our natural good; as food for hunger, and water for thirst, and sunshine for a skin starved of warmth and light, so is God to the whole appetite and aspiration of our soul. And yet we believe the tongue of the serpent, when on many occasions, grave and trivial, it tells us that by stepping into darkness we shall see, and by severance from omnipotence we shall be strong, and by revolt from our creator we shall be ourselves. And so we sympathize with the two poor mortals in the story of Eden, held down under the heel of a tyranny which consists in — what? — in walking with the King of heaven among the trees of Paradise.

Yet we cannot but feel sorry for this childish pair, who may have been petulant and foolish, and worse, ungrateful, but who by their momentary act lost happiness, and Paradise, and God. Yet it is not the fault of the Bible story to represent things so — things are so. Our foolish steps cannot be taken back: we cannot escape the consequences of our acts for ourselves or others; we sin, and our soul dies in us where we stand. And God does not suspend the natural slide of things to evil; he meets it by a more powerful and prevailing force. No one has died in Adam, who has not met, or will not meet, the life-giving power of Christ. To cover their nakedness, says the simplicity of the Old Testament, the Lord made them coats: and what does the New Testament say? Put ye on the Lord Jesus Christ; and, as we have worn the likeness of the man of clay, so shall we wear the likeness of the Man of Heaven.

21 · Called to be Saints

All accounts of the calling of saints have much in common. Compare, for example, the calling of Jeremiah according to himself (Jer. 1.4–12), and the calling of St Paul according to St Luke's memory of the Apostle's story (Acts 9). Even more striking are St Paul's own words, written to the Galatians (Gal.1.15–16): When it was the good pleasure of God, who from my mother's womb set me apart, and called me by his grace, to reveal his Son by me, that I might preach him among the nations. Compare the word of God to Jeremiah: Before I formed thee in the belly I knew thee, and before thou camest forth from the womb I sanctified thee; I have appointed thee a prophet unto the nations. It seems clear that the Apostle has been taught to see himself in Jeremiah; and this is the common rule for reading Scripture, to be on the look-out, whether God will not speak to us through his words to his servants which are written there. And it would be indeed a vain thing for us to keep the feast of St Paul's conversion, if we were not listening for what God has to say to us through it for the fulfilment of our own conversion.

'Before thou camest forth from the womb I sanctified thee.' Jeremiah's calling and St Paul's were both quite sudden; and other people were intrigued or perplexed by the violence of the change. He who once persecuted now preaches, they said of St Paul. But there is no sudden beginning about the thing as it is revealed to the men themselves. 'Before I formed thee in the belly I knew thee.' What they experience is the tearing away of all veils, the clearing of all obstacles between two things: an eternal destiny, and a field of work. Here I stand, chosen and predestined (God help me!) to publish his will. And there are the multitudes of humanity, my destined audience. That's all there is. That is all I have to consider. And Jeremiah does not say: *Me* a prophet? But, Lord, the prophets of Judah have got into a rut: they are drinking tea with the wives of the princes of Judah and speaking smooth things. There's no future in being a prophet. Nor does St Paul say: *Me* a teacher of the nations? No. They know that if there are ruts, they must jump their wheels out of them, and if there is no language in which to reach their audience, they must invent one. That is the task. The only question is, have they the strength to face it? 'Ah, Lord God, behold, I cannot speak: I am a child.' 'Say not, I am a child: to where I send thee thou shalt go, and what I command thee thou shalt speak. Be not afraid of their faces, I am with thee to deliver thee', said the Lord. Then the Lord put forth his hand and touched my mouth, and said: 'Behold, I have put my words in thy mouth. Lo, I have set thee over the nations to pluck up and pull down, to build and to plant.' The prophet was called when the first kingdom of God was falling in ruins, and the apostle was called before the new kingdom of God had taken hold. The task might be as heavy as the cross, but the issue is as clear as daylight to those blessed saints of the two Testaments, to Jeremiah and to St Paul.

22 · Providence

The tale of Rebekah's betrothal (Gen. 24) is one of those sudden unexplained decisions of which the Bible contains so many. Ruth, the Moabitess, having set out to see her widowed mother-in-law on her way home to Bethlehem, suddenly decided to go all the way with her; if she had not, Boaz would have lacked a wife, and King David a great-grandmother. And the lack of a great-grandmother is no laughing matter: one fails to get born, or, perhaps, one gets born a different person. The very idea makes one's head reel. And any Israelite might have said – indeed, might still say – Where should we be, but for Israel? And where would Israel have been without Rebekah for a mother? It was touch-and-go, after all. The mysterious old man from the other side of the sand snapped the bracelets on her wrists, and looked into her eyes: and she made up her mind. 'He wants me for his master's son; he can have me.' There was a good deal of talking afterwards, and production of marriage settlements. But the thing was already decided. What moved Rebekah? Who knows? Laban, her brother, was her guardian, and his own daughters ran away from him thirty years later; perhaps he had not the right touch with young females, and Rebekah took her chance. But the biblical writer does not probe the girl's mind. Doubtless the God of Abraham sent his angel; Rebekah did not know what she was doing, but Providence knew what he was doing with her. And it seems almost impossible not to believe in Providence, as we look back over the many apparently chance circumstances, and apparently wayward decisions, in the history of our ancestry, which have made us what we are, or even, which have made us to be at all. Heavens! What a risk you run when your great-grandmother hesitates on the steps of the chancel − it almost stops your heart to think of it − I am sure she does not know what is at stake; but the angels mean you to be, and they tip the balance of her muddled heart.

How God overrules, for his purposes, the apparent chances of life, is utterly inexplicable; even the fact of his doing so is seldom evident at the time but only afterwards. What could seem less providential than Judas' betrayal, or Peter's denial? Yet the first was the occasion of Christ's passion, by which we are all redeemed; and the second brought it about that the Church, founded on Peter, was founded on penitence, not on heroism; and so, though we are not heroes, there is hope for us all, for we can all repent. Without the control of an infinity of accidental circumstances, and even of many human follies, God would not have achieved his purpose, or established our salvation. And yet the core of it was no accident. When Christ stood unmoved before the High Priest and told him that he would meet in power the prisoner he condemned in weakness, there was no accident there, no sudden, unpredictable decision, either overruled by Providence, or swayed by the invisible touch of an angel's finger (Mark 14.62). There was a settled consistency of purpose, loyalty to the Father, love for us; this was the visible mind of Providence himself, the will that wields the world; and whatever part providential accident may have played in God's ways with us, he saves us at last by no handling of circumstance, no manipulation. We are not saved, except by the extending to us of the mind of Christ.

23 · The Outpouring

When St Mark wants to point the contrast between two stories, he sometimes uses a device – he inserts one as a sort of parenthesis into the middle of the other. In Mark 14 he inserts the story of a woman's generosity into the story of a man's meanness. The priests want an opportunity to take Jesus without the risk of riot and Judas makes a pretty sum by selling it them. Meanwhile a woman seizes the opportunity to spend her treasure in a moment's glorious waste; she cracks the alabaster, and what would have fetched three hundred crowns flows on the head which God has anointed. It is not clear that she acted with much discretion: Judas, no doubt, was far more calculating; he understood the full beauty of a scheme which would both put him on the right side of the law, and give him money in the bank. The woman merely saw before her one for whom no honour was enough, and whom no kindness would repay; she brought out the alabaster vase, and broke off the neck; she never deliberated on the alternative uses of her little store. It was Jesus who, not perhaps without a smile, made up for her surprising reasons, of which she had never dreamed: 'The poor you have always with you. . . . She did it for my burial.' 'Ah, no, alas,' she must have thought; 'and may God avert the omen of your words.'

The themes of the double story of anointing and betrayal are drawn together in the next scene, where Jesus sits at table once more among his friends. For now it is made clear that another vase is to be broken – the beautiful veined alabaster of Christ's body; and his blood is to be poured out, for his disciples to drink. It is the selfishness of Judas that is to crack the vase – 'Verily I say unto you, one of you shall betray me.' And yet with all the generosity of the woman, and infinitely more, Jesus is willing that his very blood should be emptied: he gives us the cup with his own hands 'Take, drink it,' he says, 'it is my blood.'

Moralists and philosophers bid us reflect, they would have us do the supremely reasonable thing. Our religion also bids us reflect, but not at all in the same way. We are to think once, and think twice, and think twenty times, not about our actions, but about our God: we cannot too much consider his honour, and his kindness; we may very easily consider too long just how we should respond. Christ kindles the generous heart; generosity is not a very reflective passion. The priests calculated, and Judas cashed in; the woman cracked her vase, and Jesus broke a vessel more precious to him and, in its contents, of a value no one can price.

24 · The Bread of Life

It is the spirit that quickeneth: the flesh profiteth nothing: the words that I speak unto you, they are spirit, and they are life (John 6.63).

In the discourse on the Bread of Life our Saviour makes two points. First, his disciples must eat his flesh and drink his blood, in plain, physical, sacramental fact. If they do this they will become one body with him and will share his life. He does not develop this point, he simply states it. Why the sacramental act gives us a share in his life is a mystery about which he says nothing. It appears that the sign is left to speak for itself. What is eating after all? To eat is to appropriate the substance of what one eats: if we eat the flesh and drink the blood of the Son of Man, we shall receive our part of what he is. Leaving, then, the sacramental act to be its own explanation, Christ proceeds to another point. The flesh of the Son of Man, in which they share, is the vehicle of immortal life, and if they share in it they too will live for ever. This point he does proceed to develop. If the flesh of the Son of Man is immortal and life-giving, it is not because it is a peculiar or magical sort of flesh. It is just flesh as ours is, of its own nature liable to corruption. But it is indwelt by a spirit, which is a life almighty and divine, and which will not allow it to perish; and this will be revealed when, presently, Jesus rises from the tomb and ascends up, where he was before; that is, returns to the God from whom he came. When they see this, his disciples will not doubt that there is in him a spirit which is the power of immortal life.

Moreover, he says, the *words* that I speak to you, they are spirit, they are life. Consider what he says. The words of Jesus, like anyone else's words, are sounds in his disciples' ears; to take a step back, they are vibrations in the air, or, to go further back still, they are movements of his tongue and throat. They too, so far, are flesh and not spirit: they are, indeed, something less than flesh, they are slight and transitory motions of fleshly organs. But being this, they are the action of his will: the action of a mind which neither lies nor repents. When he says that he is the bread come down from heaven, his whole being is in the saying of this; he means it with all he is, and he puts all that he is into the saying of it: he commits himself to the giving of himself on the cross, for our everlasting nourishment. The word of Jesus is the unqualified act of his spirit – there is no discount to be allowed – it is not more or less he, it is *he*. The utterance is transitory – the tongue is silent, the vibration dies – but the spirit is immortal, for it is one with the will which made all things, older than the mountains, more durable than the stars: a wellspring of being and life inexhaustible, which first gave to us, and will everlastingly renew to us, this person which we are.

Jesus unites himself with his disciples on both levels, both in flesh and in spirit. He takes our flesh from Mary, and so he has a tongue to speak, a hand to bless, and a heart to break. And his disciples take him in flesh, too: they eat the flesh of the Son of Man, they drink his blood, in physical fact; and if this eating and drinking is a crude and simple thing, so is the birth of Jesus, and his sucking at the breast, a crude simple thing. By such means he became ours, by such means we became his. But he unites himself with his disciples, too, on the level of spirit, and does this by his words. 'If ye abide in me,' he says, 'and my *words* abide in you, ye shall ask what ye will. . . .' He says, 'I am the Bread that came down from heaven', and his saying it is eternal Spirit. We receive the word, and say with faith: 'Thou are the Bread that cometh down from heaven', and our saying it is eternal Spirit. For this is faith: faith is a divine gift; faith is the extension of the will, act and mind of Jesus in us.

25 · The Bugle-Call

Don't you find the prophecy of Ezekiel (ch. 33) somewhat intimidating? Or perhaps it is not quite so intimidating for you as it is for me. For I have to suspect that, though I am no prophet nor son of a prophet, nevertheless I am a watchman. God does not desire souls to perish, but they may; and he has laid it on his ministers to warn them. He has given us a bugle to blow; and though we are not to blow it unless he bids us, yet if he bids us, and we do not blow, then it will be better for us if we had never been born. Here indeed is a subject for our self-examination.

Perhaps, though, it is not quite the same under the New Testament as it was under the Old. The business of the ancient prophets was to give different warnings from time to time, as God commanded them. But our business, now Christ has come, is to say always the same thing: 'Neglect not so great a salvation.' Yet the will of God for your salvation comes to bear on your life at different points from day to day; so we have still to enquire into the mind of the Lord, and see if he has any special note for us to sound.

Ezekiel speaks of warnings in general but St John gives

us one warning in particular: the love of God cannot be separated from the love of man. If a man say, I love God, and hateth his brother, he is a liar — or, as we might say, he is a hypocrite. For he that loveth not the brother whom he hath seen, cannot love God, whom he hath not seen (I John 4. 20). Ah, you say, how true! How true! This is the stuff! Down with supernatural religion! Christianity is sheer kindness! Well, it isn't: nor does St John say it is. He says you cannot love God *unless* you love your brother; he does not say you need not love God — God who has shown what love is, by the way in which he has first loved us. But we will let that point go for the present, and stick to sheer human kindness. Is there a note in Ezekiel's bugle which sounds for us specially, a direction about the practice of kindness?

Christ, the judge and everlasting shepherd, says he will place on his right hand those who feed the hungry, clothe the naked, and visit the prisoners or the sick. It is not such people who, at the moment, mainly hold out their hands for your help. But there are among you the less forthcoming, the less well-friended, the less happy; every society has such members, often the most original and, in the end, with most to contribute to us. But a superficial and callous social judgement holds them cheap. It is a serious temptation of young people to let friendship be corrupted with ambition: to want to know the best people and to succeed with those whom all admire. We are ashamed to be thought to go about with companions whom our friends do not value, and we join our voices to the depreciation of them behind their back. And anyhow, we do not want to be bored. No: but these are also the children of God; and he who loves the Father will love also the Son he has begotten. Need I say more? The contribution you can make to others' happiness — not to mention your own — by keeping an eye open for people without a ready-made social life — who can estimate it? But I cannot get the right words: you are not to patronize anyone; you are just to free yourself from your own prejudice and folly, and see people as they are.

Loving our brother, we may love God also: and Christ gave us a perfect means to join the two sorts of love, when he gave us a table, at which we might share together the bread of God. In this most serious and most kind of Christian actions the faith of each is sustained by the faith of all: the body of Christ must be put together entire out of all its members at every weekly communion, and no part be lacking. I am not telling you that you may come unprepared, for you know you must not. But why should you ever be unprepared? Why shouldn't you acknowledge, and embrace, the known will of God every week, and make confession to him who is most faithful and just in the forgiving of sins?

26 · The Word of God

The development of St John's visions in his great Revelation, the way in which one scene grows out of another, is as wonderful as the visions themselves. Though you may not be great in the art of devout meditation, you have sometimes thought about God, or about some text in the Bible, and have discovered for yourself how divine truth spreads and moves in the mind, how one thought gives rise to another. And when this happens, you will humbly believe that the Spirit of God is at work, revealing the things of God. It was St John's privilege that his thoughts became visions, full of the immediate presence of divine things; but even though they came so powerfully alive, they were still thoughts, and we can watch them expand, as thoughts do, under the influence of his inspiration.

Trace, in Revelation 19, the development of a single idea. St John is present, in his vision, at the worship of heaven; and that, indeed, is nothing strange, for it is in the presence of angels and archangels that the Christian at all times gives to his Lord God the thanks that are meet and right. St John hears the praises of the angel choirs; then he hears the heavenly elders saying Amen, it is truth. Amen: a familiar word, asserting that what we say of God is what God has said of himself, and that it is true. Amen: it is the response to *all* the words of God; and presently St John hears another divine utterance through the lips of an angel: Blessed are they that are bidden to the marriage-supper of the Lamb. Once more a heavenly tongue adds the Amen to it, but this time the Amen is paraphrased and spread out: the angel says not 'Amen' but, These words are true words of God. These words, says the angel, which I have uttered are not mine, they are the very words of God. It seems only right to St John that he should fall in worship before the self-confessed mouthpiece of God; but no, says the angel, not to me: I am only your fellow-servant. Are not you yourself a prophet, and a mouthpiece of God, able to speak his very words, and say Amen to them, too? Worship God.

Worship God? But where is he, that I should worship him? In what face may I meet his very look, what hand may I kiss for his? If that is St John's question, his next vision answers it. There are angels, there are prophets who report the words of God and say Amen to them; but there is one who is the Word of God, the expression of his mind in flesh and blood. See, the heavens rend, and he rides forth crowned with diadem, carrying the title, Word of God. He is all that God has to say; and it needs no other to attest with an Amen *what* he says, for his life and person are his attestation: his very name is not only Word of God but also Faithful and True: we remember that 'true word of God' was the angel's paraphrase for 'Amen': look, it has clothed itself in flesh and blood. We have advanced from 'Amen' to true words of God and from true words of God to one called 'faithful and true' and titled 'Word of God'. Here then is the true 'Amen' whose very life is his attestation. His life? Much more his death: he is the martyr, faithful and true, as he shows us by his garment, sprinkled with his blood.

No word of God is void of power, for by the word of the Lord the heavens were made; but here the heavens rend to let out the Word of God, riding to conquer the earth. This warrior is almighty, but he is not unsupported; the hosts of heaven ride after him clothed in white linen, that is, in the merits of their sanctity. They are white robed, his coat is spattered with blood; for by his sacrifice they are purified. They fight his battle, the saints fight with Christ; their martyrdom carries the sword of his passion into every corner of the field, his love speaks in their love, his prayer in their prayers. This is the army that fights from heaven, God in Christ, Christ in the saints; and we, in our battle, have fellowship with them. The saints are inseparable from Christ, for apart from him they have no being: they are one act of love with him, their hearts are in it when for our rescue the Son of God goes forth to war.

27 · Praying for Others

You often want to know what good it does for us to pray, since we can scarcely hope that God will change his mind to oblige us, nor, indeed, that the world would be any better off if he did. If that is your objection, it is worth your while to notice how much ammunition the Bible provides for it. Balaam (Num. 22–24) had a great reputation for effective prayer: whom he blessed was blessed, whom he prayed against was frustrated; so when the King of Moab saw a new and dangerous tribe camping on his borders he sent for Balaam to pray against them, much as, in time of war, the Queen's government expects the Church to pray against the Queen's enemies. But Balaam met an angel with a drawn sword, where he could not get past him without riding through him; and the angel would not let him go alive, except on the promise of making no prayers but as God should direct.

You might expect the moral of the story to be that prayer is vain: if Israel, blessed by God, cannot be cursed, it is as useless, though not so impious, for Balaam to bless as for Balaam to ban. But that is not the moral of the story.

69

The King of Moab lamented because his hired intercessor had turned the sword of the spirit against his own breast in blessing his enemies. The conclusion is not, because God has blessed Israel, Balaam need not, but, because God has blessed them, Balaam must.

It often seems to us that tyrannical governments usurp the prerogatives of God himself, and in nothing so much as in this, that they are not content with the silence or acquiescence of their subjects; not to be vocal in the ruler's cause is itself a crime. It is a blasphemous tyranny to require such worship of one's fellow humans, but for God to require it of his creatures is inevitable and right. God has cursed the works of the devil, and we must curse them: God has blessed our friends, and shall not we bless them with a faithful heart and an incessant voice? Shall not we relay the blessing and the ban which spring out of the heart that made the world? If you say, What need has omnipotence of my heart's support, I will ask you, What need omnipotence has of your hand's assistance? Yet I suppose you do not mean to sit with your hands in your lap: you know that religion is mere hypocrisy if we do not do the will of God. Never say, Can I move God by my prayers? But always reflect: The blessings of God are piling against my door. Up, open and let in the avalanche of gold. Some will remain in my house with me, some will pass on through me to other hands. Ah, no, the division is false: no blessings so securely remain as those which pass on, for how can I be more blessed myself than in blessing my friends out of the heart and mouth of God?

28 · The Spirit and the Name

What did our Saviour mean by the mysterious and disturbing words, 'Blasphemy against the Holy Ghost shall not be forgiven: it is an everlasting sin' (Mark 3.29)?

I begin by saying that Christ did not make up, or introduce for the first time, the doctrine of irremissible guilt in connection with blasphemy. It was a part of the Jewish religion, and they reckoned to find it in scripture. The divine voice had declared to them from Sinai, I will not hold him guiltless, that takes my Name in vain. Now Christ's method of teaching the Jews was not to contradict the scripture, but to interpret it. He says to them therefore: This sin of blasphemy which is so grave, what is it? Is it committed when one lightly and thoughtlessly pronounces the Name of God, if one ventures even to use that most holy Name which Jews write but never read out, unless it be the High Priest once a year, blessing Israel on the Day of Atonement? Is that the sin? Why then, we might fall into such sin almost without knowing it. It seems that, if we are to blaspheme the Name of God in any serious sense, we must know what we do, we must be right up against the

71

power and majesty of the Name. When does that happen? There may be grave danger of its happening in the case of which Jesus speaks (Mark 3.22). If the Name of God is used to cast out evil and to heal the mind, if in the Name of God Jesus bids demons begone, and they go, if the Name shows its power, and is accompanied by the manifest action of the Holy Ghost, then those who blaspheme and call the power of God the power of Satan blaspheme indeed. That is what I take to be our Lord's teaching. If you want to know whether our Saviour meant that this sin, once committed, would sink the soul everlastingly in the pit of hell, without remedy, I must say that I cannot believe it, any more than I suppose you can. And why? Because, though many sins of their own nature have eternal effect and kill the soul, Christ who said these words was going himself to die in order that sinners might repent and live. I take it that when he spoke of irremissible sin, he meant, irremissible if unrepented and unconfessed. But it is not this point that I want to pursue. What interests me is that Christ associated himself with the Jewish reverence for the Name of God, and connected the living use of God's Name with the presence of the Holy Ghost. For that connection is the premise of his whole argument: where the Name of God is truly invoked, there is the Holy Spirit. What does this doctrine mean? I will put it in my own way.

God dwells in us: that is the supreme mercy which we adore at Whitsuntide. And how does he dwell in us? In two ways, by his Spirit and by his Name. First, by his Spirit: he dwells in us personally and invisibly, the infinite God, deep under the root of our heart, constantly active to insert his inspirations wherever we do not frustrate him by our selfishness and inattention. We carry him with us, or rather, wherever we go he carries us, and we do not know it. Then, second, he dwells in us by his Name: it is thus he inhabits our conscious mind. Where would God be in all our thoughts if his Name were not there to stand for him? What are our minds indeed but piles of images and words, together with the mysterious power of spelling them out into thoughts? A mind in which the Name of God is present is a very different thing from a mind in which that Name finds no place. What can I do, indeed, to make God the master in the house of my mind, but to enthrone his Name in the midst of all the words my memory contains, and that this blessed Name should be spilled into all the sentences where it ought to belong, and determine the sense of them? What is a God-possessed mind, but a mind whose words and thoughts turn constantly about the Name of God? For when the Name of God so reigns among the words of our inward speech, then the Spirit of God which is God himself finds an entry and shines like a glory round that blessed Name, spreading love and faith and every virtue.

Those who designed this chapel made the alms dish to stand in the middle of the altar, according to the custom of those times, and embossed upon it the sacred monogram of Jesus surrounded by a glory, which is the light of the Spirit of God breaking forth from the Name. Jesus, himself all-holy, invoked the Name of God to cast out demons from the hearts of others, and there was seen the operation of the Holy Ghost. But I will invoke the Name to cast the demons out of my own heart, and then too I will have faith in the operation of the Holy Ghost. And, that the Name may keep its power and radiance for others and for me, I ask first of all petitions in the Lord's Prayer for the grace to hallow it, both on my lips and in my mind, by thought, and word and deed. For he who taught us to fear the blasphemy of the Holy Ghost taught us also thus to pray: Father, hallowed be thy Name.

29 · Facing Christ

What is the Christian faith, reduced to a single fact? Is it not that we are actually in the same world with a living Christ? Does not everything else come down to this, or spring from this? It is important, certainly, on the one side to know what Christ is, and by what steps or acts he came to stand where he now stands; and on the other side to know what he does to us by being in one world with us. But if it is a matter of experiencing our faith, it is enough to be set face to face with Christ; for if we come face to face with him, we shall know what he is, and if he shows himself to us, he will do to us what he does.

In the first chapters of his Revelation, St John experiences Jesus Christ as a presence of unbearable power and radiance – unbearable, that is, to mere humanity, but made both bearable and sweet by his grace. His voice was as the voice of many waters, and from his mouth a sharp two-edged sword went forth; his countenance was as the sun shineth in his strength. When I saw him, I fell before his feet as dead. But he laid his right hand upon me, saying, Fear not, I am the first and the last: I am the living one who died, and lo, am alive for ever, and hold the keys of death and hell.

He died, and lives; and now his presence both kills and makes alive again, and an illimitable energy of life and death continues to act through the words he speaks to the churches. He kills them with his warnings, and brings them back to life with his promises. The modern reader, trained to a code of silken manners, and inclined to make Godhead in the image of what he reckons human, is shocked, or at least disquieted, at the sword-thrusts of the Son of Man, threatening his frail disciple even with death. But this is not a question of manners: this is how his pure judgement bears on their infidelities and on ours. But if his judgement is unsparing, his promises are breathtaking: To him that overcometh I will give to eat of the tree of life, which is in the garden of God. Be faithful to death: I will give thee the crown of life. He judges us as we dare not judge ourselves, he promises us what we could not dream of promising ourselves, but, more amazing yet, he honours us as we dare not in our most foolish vanity honour ourselves. I know your works – Ah, Lord, then we may say, covering our eyes, forget them – but he proceeds: I know your works, your effort and endurance, your impatience of villainy. Or again, I know how you are placed, where Satan's throne is, yet you hold my name fast, and have not denied my faith, even in the days when Antipas, my faithful witness, was slain amongst you, where Satan's home is. And is not this worse than the judgement, the most heartbreaking thing of all, that he so prizes what we have done well, and that we have thought so little of it, and given him so little of what he so dearly loves?

30 · Baptism of a Child

No one who witnesses these venerable ceremonies can doubt of one thing. The baptism of an infant is an anticipation of adult faith. In a way that is touching to believers and absurd to unbelievers, we treat the child as a person, a self-conscious, responsible child of God. But then, that is how we believe that God works. The tenses of the verb are of little importance in the view of eternity: God sees from the beginning to the end. Before this child was born, or conceived, God's mercy had received him. When Christ died on the cross, this boy was redeemed by the infinite worth of precious blood. Now, at the font, he is taken into the stream of divine action; his salvation will be achieved day by day, and completed when he sees the face of God. Not one of us is really a different case. If, in baptism, this child is viewed as an adult, so we, who are sinners, trust to be received as saints in the eyes of that compassion which redeems us. We are living members of Christ. We are, in God's foresight, what his love will one day make us.

But the merciful imputation of a future perfection is not

a pretence; God knows how he will sanctify us, when he accepts us as saints; and he knows how he will make this child a Christian, in accepting him as such. He knows that he means to use you, his parents; and I know you would not have been so frivolous or so sacrilegious as to bring this child to baptism, unless you were fully resolved, as far as in you lies, to make him the Christian which God sees in him. Every such dear responsibility, every such personal tie, gives a new meaning and importance to our own religion. One's own soul may seem cheap, though it did not, to him who died for it, but none of us lives to self alone, none dies to self alone. The birth of your son is the rebirth of your love for God, who entrusted you with so infinite a treasure.

The salvation of this child, like the salvation of us all, lies in the infinite life of God, and in his inexhaustible kindness, made present to us in our Saviour, poured out in his sacrifice, and joined to us by the link of our baptism. To strengthen this link, to open this channel, is the whole practice of our religion, and in case the claim of God on our own heads should lose its force − and such is our perversity, it can − he gives us one another, our friends, our children into our keeping, and bids us open ourselves to him, that through us he may come at them. And so, through the love we bear to them, he persuades us to love him.

31 · Greater than our Hearts

The strange legend of the Flood (Gen. 6–8) carries more weight in its introductory phrases than it does in all the picturesque detail of the event; for here it is that we read the words: The Lord saw that the wickedness of man was great upon the earth, and that every imagination of the thought of his heart was only evil continually. And it repented the Lord that he had made man on the earth, and it grieved him to the heart. This text has played a greater part than any other in the development of the doctrine, or rather the discovery, that the human heart is corrupted, and sick at the root. But more significant still is the connection the text makes between the corruption of the human heart and the grieving of God's.

The story goes on to tell us that God washed the world of its wickedness by a flood, and then vowed he would never do so again. Why? because people were never to be wicked again? Alas, no. Then why? Because of God's own heart. Yet the story seems unfinished. Wickedness needs to be washed away; yet the love of God forbids him to repeat so drastic a remedy. Is humankind then, to be wicked, and is God to grieve?

What the old religion could not solve, the new made clear. According to the New Testament, the world is washed by a more efficacious flood, poured from the very heart of God made man; the very heart which grieves for our corrupted heart is ripped open on the cross, and pours water and blood; and this, sacramentally considered, is the water of baptism, a flood which washes away not sinners, but their sin.

Now, says St John in his epistle, when we Christians take up the old text, and read about the corrupt heart of humanity, and the grieving heart of God, our own heart will still condemn us on many accounts, for sloth, selfishness, vanity. . . . There is the old corruption, and there is the grief for it in the heart of God. Yet, says St John, whereinsoever our heart condemn us, we shall assure our hearts before God. And why? Because (and this seems a strange reason) God is greater than our heart, and knoweth all things. God is greater than our heart: that is, he is a higher authority, and though our heart condemn us, he can absolve us. But why should he absolve us? Because (and this seems a stranger reason still) he knoweth all things. But if God knows all things, he has all the more reason to condemn me, since he knows even what I manage to hide from myself. Ah, but that is to take too narrow a view of what God knows — he knows all things, not merely what I have done or thought amiss, but what he has designed for my justification and my glory. He sees me caught up in the stream of his great purposes, carried away in that flood which burst forth from the heart of Jesus Christ. And, says St John, he has given me tokens of the truth that he has floated me away on that saving tide — the acts of Christian love that he enables me to do, the evidence of his heart in my heart. Hereby we know we love, because he laid down his life for us.... Let us love not in word, not in tongue, but in deed and in truth.... Hereby shall we know that we are of the truth, and shall assure our hearts before him, whereinsoever our heart condemn us: for God is greater than our heart, and knoweth all things – he knows, that is, the secret channel by which the love of his Son who laid down his life for us has run into the root of our heart and become the love we bear towards our brethren. And so, though our heart condemn us, yet, on a better view, it will not condemn us: for who am I to condemn what God absolves? And, if our heart condemn us not, then have we boldness towards God. And whatsoever things we ask we receive of him.

32 · The Living God

An American and a Japanese fell into conversation. The American, with more frankness than tact, was pressing the Japanese about the Emperor-cult. This little palace-dweller in spectacles – who could believe that he was descended from gods, and who could believe, anyway, in the sort of native gods from whom he was said to be descended? Who could take seriously the supposition that there was divine ichor in Mikado's veins or that the existence of the Japanese people was bound up with the safety of his sacred person, or that his expressed wishes were heavenly oracles? The Japanese was inclined at first to put a firm, if bland, face upon the matter and say simply, 'We believe it, though you do not believe it.' Then, smiling a little conspiratorially in sympathy with the mockery he saw in the American's eye, he said: What, after all, is the urgency of the question? If the Emperor is not divine, if he is, indeed, not even a man but a hollow statue, what difference will it make? We shall continue to bow towards him and to fulfil the etiquette of court and government as though in his omniscient sight. We shall give our lives, if need be, for the sacred throne as we have always done, and the empire will be saved — if the sacrifice of our lives can save it, he added, thinking of that mushroom of smoke that once hung over the Japanese sky.

Such, continued the Japanese, is the nature of religion. The moving power is in our hearts: the gods save us by awakening and focusing our measureless respect, and to do so they need not actually have existed. You Christians now — he said, smiling a little more broadly — I would not presume to deny that your religion is as good as ours. You have a divine-human monarch, enthroned not on earth, but in heaven. Permit me to say that from a purely Japanese point of view the distance to be covered in a visit to court must be somewhat inconvenient; but you, it seems, do not find it to be so, and when you turn towards his celestial abode you are moved with unbounded respect for his person and his wishes, and inclined — so you tell me — towards the performance of all the laudable duties. That is an admirable result, but I do not see that it is dependent on his actually existing, especially as he does not have, like our Mikado, to satisfy the test of being occasionally visible. Everything would go on as it is going on, if he had never actually performed those edifying acts of self-devotion in Jerusalem, of which the thought has so salutary an effect on your wills. For it is your wills, I take it, that turn the mill of Christendom, as it is our will here that moves the levers of the imperial machine.

The American was confused by this attack, and too ashamed to reply. How true, he said to himself as he went off, how true of most of us! How well he has described the Christianity of politicians and, indeed, of eighty or ninety per cent called Christians among us! Certainly he has left something out — certainly our formal Christendom leaves something out, as we nod our heads before our heavenly Mikado and trust our own reverence and strength to turn the wheels of the world.

What have we left out? Death, and the Holy Ghost. Death: for when we come to die, I think, no moving power in our own hearts or wills is going to raise us from our dust. We shall be dead; and the difference between a real God and an edifying fiction will then be plain, for no edifying fiction raises the dead. Death, and the Holy Ghost: for we have been taught that if ever we are to have that everlasting life which no mortal dust can give to itself, we must begin to live by it here and now. And what we cannot achieve being dead, we cannot achieve either in a mortal life. We must be born again. What we cannot love, we *must* love; and what we cannot experience, we must believe; and what we cannot be, we must be made. Now therefore you who gave us creation, you who must give us resurrection, do not delay, but according to Christ's most faithful promise, God living and true, dove, wind, and tongues of fire, come, Holy Ghost: do with us what you will, oh God of terror, God of peace.

33 · A Person's Worth

Our founder's motto, If you want a secret kept, trust it to no one — *quod tacitum velis, nemini dixeris* — is characteristic of his age and generation: it is in accord with the wariness, the 'I'm not buying it' expression which looks at us out of the eyes of our Tudor portraits. Common interest, says Ecclesiasticus, is a better basis for friendship than common pleasure; but it would be better not to trust any friend who has any conceivable temptation for letting you down. No doubt there is a paragon, if you can find him, the godly man, pure gold through and through. But take good care you have got him before you confide in him (Ecclus. 6.1–17).

Here's a rascal for you, said Philemon to St Paul. I called his Onesimos when I bought him, but Onesimos — a profitable investment — that's just what he isn't. Anyone can have him, for me. You can have him, if you like, to carry your bags; but don't you trust him an inch. Off they went, the Apostle and his slave, and the trip proved unexpectedly long: round by Macedonia into Greece — that was planned, and so was the dash to Jerusalem, in time for Pentecost, but not the riot in the temple, nor the long months and years of waiting for the case to be tried. Having settled in a Roman prison, St Paul felt it was about time he returned Philemon's loan, which he did, in a letter expressing such a conflict of emotions that it's almost unintelligible. It's about time I sent him back (so writes the Apostle). If he was yours before, by honest purchase, he's doubly so now, by common membership in Jesus Christ, for I've made a son of him here in my prison. So here he is, a piece of my heart: receive him as me – he's all the me I can let you have, at the moment, being chained up here – but I'll come soon, I'll come. Meanwhile here's Onesimos, here's a bit of Paul for you – yes, I suppose you will want to keep him, he's yours – but then, how about my having a bit of Philemon in prison here with me? I'm an old man now: if Onesimos looks after me, it's as though you did it. My dear man, I don't know what to say – but you see what I want: I won't ask, but I know you'll do it. If he owes you any old debts or has anything to work off with you, score it against me, I'll pay it – not to mention that you owe me, who brought you to Christ, your own soul anyway.

What a letter! What a mixture of passions! What a confusion of persons! Paul, Philemon, and the much-whipped slave merging into one another and taken for one another; because all of them, the persecutor, the slave and the slave-master, are one in Christ and have to be taken as Christ. To know what is the worth of various persons is certainly a sort of wisdom, and such was the wisdom of the ancient Jew. To know how to share with others a worth which neither they nor we possess, is another sort of wisdom; and such was the wisdom of Christ's Apostle. And such, perhaps, has been the wisdon of several people who have had you and me in hand, on occasions in our lives that we can remember, if we bother to try.

34 · The Light of Christ

That Christ healed the blind, I make no doubt: even Christian saints, and some others not such saints either, have performed cures by a spiritual power going beyond anything we can explain. The old theologians used to say, 'He suffered as man, he healed as God', but we might prefer to say that his healing was a combination, like all his other acts, of the human and the divine: it was a human gift made the instrument of God in flesh.

The evangelist is anxious to show us that *this* healing (John 9) is beyond all human record: since the world was, who ever heard of a man's eyes opened, that had been born blind? He is no less anxious for us to see that the healing of the eyes was the symbol of a spiritual restoration: the blind man saw not the physical face of Jesus only, he also saw in that face the Son of God. The Pharisees, refusing to see anything divine in so evident a miracle, condemn themselves to self-inflicted blindness. So far as the man was concerned, his obtaining of sight and his seeing of God were so united that we can scarcely separate them by a hair's breadth; as in the Sacrament of the altar, the sign and the grace signified are absolutely one. For his seeing of God was in his experience of God's love, and the divine love he experienced was the gift of his sight; what he was physically made to see was the face of Jesus, and what he spiritually discerned was the divinity behind those eyes.

Sight, light, illumination are constant metaphors of grace: and the metaphor itself is many-sided. For first, we are in the dark about God, and the whole world of things acts as a screen of darkness we cannot penetrate, and God is above, behind, within. But then second, we are in the dark about this world, for we can see none of it as it is, and especially we can see no fellow-humans as they are until we learn to see them through the eyes of God. Third, we are in the dark about our way, not knowing what path to follow, like wanderers in a jungle; for only the sheer shining of God's will can tell us what is our calling in life, and what tracks are to be shunned, what explored. But fourth, we are in the dark, a sad darkness has invaded us and settled upon us; we do not know what it is to live in the light, until we are turned to God and engaged in doing his will for the love of him. Then the worldly world, and our own will and eyes, shine with a beautiful clearness which is the climate of heaven. In all these ways the grace of God is light. I am the light of the world, says the Lord. He that pleaseth me shall not walk in darkness, but shall have the light of life. And, he warns us, while you have the light, walk by the light, that ye may become children of light. For, indeed, the night cometh when no one can walk, or work; and it will be time to see what use we have made of the day.

35 · The People of God

The people who heard St Peter speak put themselves into his hands (Acts 2). They were pricked to the heart, and said to him, What are we to do? It was St Peter's first missionary sermon. You may wonder whether he had foreseen the eventuality, or whether he had any formula ready prepared. Think of it: if you are consistent Christians, whose life witnesses your faith, it may happen to you some time, that one of your friends, whose godless world has suddenly crumbled, will put himself into your hands. 'I want to be a Christian: what am I to do?' Perhaps you won't take the job on yourself. You will think swiftly of the most reliable guide you know, the most likely to sympathize with your friend, the most likely to convince his reason, and to warm his heart. St Peter had no such resources to fall back upon. It was only yesterday, and he would have referred the enquirers to Jesus; but now, there he stood, unsupported by any human authority. He was armed with the Spirit of Jesus, and he had to act; he had to tell them what to do.

He told them to repent, to be baptized, and to look for

the gift of the Holy Ghost. They renounced their sins, they accepted the baptismal water, they began to rely on the inspiration of the God within. But that was not all; the pattern of saving action continued to work itself out, and in the next verses we read: They were steady in their attendance on the Apostles' teaching; for they had still much to learn about the man, the God, who had died for them. They were regular in fellowship, sharing the broken bread; there they prayed together. Also there sprang up between them the closest bond of charity, they could not have enough of one another's company; and they could not bear that any should be in need, while they had money to give, or possessions to sell.

That was the Christian pattern, first made by the Holy Ghost, and there is no reason to suppose that Christianity will survive the loss of it. An apostolic authority round which to rally; a society bound together equally by sacramental practice, by friendship and by charitable kindness; a reverential fear for the God who sets up his throne in every Christian breast, in my neighbour's as much as in mine, and in the whole mind of the Church above all. Go then, and find the Church, wherever you are, and do your part to work her pattern. The God within you will not retain his throne, unless you let him hold together the provinces of his empire, and keep your life at one with the lives of his believing people.

36 · Voices of the Spirit

Palestine had two harvests: corn at Pentecost, wine and oil at the feast of Tabernacles. The Israelites made their thanksgiving at both seasons and at the same time remembered those great historical actions through which the Lord God had made them possessors of corn, wine and oil, delivering them from Egypt, leading them through the wilderness, and overthrowing the Canaanite before their face. But on the day of Pentecost they remembered more especially an event which had happened (they were assured) about the Pentecostal season. In the course of their journey from Egypt to the land of corn, wine and oil, the tribes of Jacob had camped at the foot of Sinai, about the end of May. The volcanic mountain was clothed in fire, and in the thunderous roar they had heard the voice of God, making covenant with them, and binding them under the terms of his law. Never, the pious Israelite believed, had God been so near to his people as on that day, when they saw his great fire, and heard his glorious voice. He could not so remain among them — human flesh was too frail to bear it — but he had given them a token of his presence, to remain forever in their hearts, the ten words, his holy commandments, through which the Spirit of God should be visibly displayed, moulding the life and conduct of his people.

'And that's just fine for you,' said the Jew's Gentile friend, hearing him tell this pious story; 'but where do we come in? That's what I'd like to know. Your God seems to have gone in for racial discrimination in a big way; but now he's behind the times. Our Lord the Emperor is not so exclusive: he extends the privileges of a Roman Peace to all mankind; all races begin to share in the Roman Law.' 'You have got hold of the wrong end of the stick, as usual', the Jew replied, 'for our Rabbis teach that when the voice of the Holy One (blessed be he!) issued forth from the cloud of his glory, it was parted into seventy voices, expressed in seventy languages, and distributed to the seventy races of mankind, as though through seventy interpreters; but there were no interpreters: the Holy One who can do all things, himself spoke seventyfold. The king of the whole world taught with his breath: but in sixty-nine tongues he spoke in vain, for not an ear was open to hear. Only the seventieth voice, speaking our Hebrew language found an audience, for our fathers had prepared their hearts, and Moses had exhorted them.'

Let us suppose that this typical interchange between Jew and Gentile takes place at Jerusalem at the Pentecost of AD30. There are, obviously, several points of objection and reply still needing to be developed, and the conversation might trail inconclusively for some time, if it were not interrupted by a noise: twelve men running out of a neighbouring house into the street and shouting for joy. They are not masters of themselves: the glory which possesses them is beyond articulate utterance: it tumbles from their throats in an ecstasy of rhythmical sound. It is easy to say that they are drunk – though it's somewhat early in the day – it is easy to say it, if you are free to say it; but our Jew, and our Gentile, find that they are not free to say this, for, in common with a medley of several nations, collected at Jerusalem by the feast, they are enraptured: they stand with streaming eyes and upturned faces, to hear the voice of the Spirit. For the same power which possesses the speakers invades their hearers, and interprets to their hearts the message of apostolic ecstasy. In the formulation which is most intimate and familiar to each – in the words each learnt from the mother who nursed him – they conceive the sense of that torrential praise: it is a hymn which glorifies the wonderful works of a present God. Here the legend of Sinai becomes fact: the divine voice pours abroad, and is distributed without interpreters to people of many nations. But now, in the new Pentecost, the nations hearken; now the voice of God issues not from the mountain top of fire, but from the lips of those on whom a spiritual fire has come down. Then it was law that spoke, but now it is song and exultation, and everlasting joy. Peter, at length recovering the mastery of his voice, begins in clear words to tell them what it is, to cite ancient prophecies and new miracles.

On this day the Church was effectively born, born of ecstasy and possession, glorying to live the life of resurrection by the power of God. The passage of years has sobered our mood, but it has not changed our faith: we that are baptized into Christ still have within us the fountain of living water, the mind of the Spirit, the heart of God. Uncover the well, release the waters: it is God himself who rises in our hearts and praises God; we wait for his loving kindness, we listen for it: the God within lifts us to the God above.

37 · The Service of God

There can be few more selfless tasks in the literary line than the composition of a gospel. Any biographer is bound to keep himself out of the picture, and leave us face to face with his hero. How much more an evangelist: for what impertinence could be greater than to obtrude oneself between one's readers, and the voice, or the face, of the Son of God. The more self-effacing of modern biographers often present us with a mosaic of their subject's letters; St Luke's mosaic is of Christ's conversation. He shows his art, nevertheless, in the arrangement of the pieces, and it is by appreciating this that we can penetrate the evangelist's incognito, and know his thoughts.

The parable of the Good Samaritan (Luke 10.25–37) has a straightforward moral. The priest and the Levite were on their way to or from Jerusalem, the scene of their sacred duties, and these Israelite characters might surely be thought to have their feet on the heavenly road. And yet, with their noses towards heaven and their ears buttoned up, they missed the chance of a lifetime, to save a fellow creature from present pain and probable death. They left the job to a profane man and a heretic, whose heart was in the right place: *he was moved with compassion.* So, it seems, one can have too much religion; or else, to put it differently, religion is not in the Temple, it is in the place of human need.

We might conclude, broadening the moral, that kindness is the only creed. But St Luke won't have this, either. I told you that he shows his cunning in the arrangement of his pieces; and no sooner have we had the picture of the Good Samaritan's hospitality, paying the bill for the man whose purse was gone, than we are presented with the figure of the bustling, hospitable Martha. What entertainment can be good enough for the Saviour of the world? Why does not Mary help? Why not? because one dish will do; and it is folly to fuss about housekeeping, when you might be learning from the lips of Truth himself. So sometimes the conventions of common kindness should be set aside, that we may seize the heart of religion; just as, at other times, the conventions of piety should be forgotten, that we may obey the heart of mercy. The art of life cannot be taught by rule; we must have an open ear for the living voice of God, which calls us variously on various occasions: here, to acts of kindness; there, to worship and a quiet waiting on God.

So we may begin to respect St Luke's wisdom, or rather, his appreciation of Christ's. But we are not at the end of his evangelist's subtleties. For, if we turn back to the text on which the parable of the Samaritan hangs, we see that it is the great commandment of love to God and one's neighbour. The scribe's question, And who is my neighbour? draws from Christ the parable of the Samaritan. We look for something in comment on the duty to love God, by way of balance, and are not disappointed. One thing is needful: Mary hath chosen the good part which shall not be taken from her. True, the one comment is a parable from Christ's lips, the other an incident from his life. But here again is something St Luke might wish his readers to consider. Jesus is the living Word of God: his speech and action are one. In grace and in simplicity, he talks and he lives the love both of God and of neighbour.

38 · Instruments of God

There is something a little disquieting about the Wise Man's pious remarks on the medical art, and its relation to the healing power of God. We know, of course, that medicine in his day did not inspire the confidence it now does; a point which comes out forcibly in the verse immediately following the end of the lesson, and no doubt very prudently cut by our lectionary: 'He that offends against his Maker, let him fall into the hands of his doctor.' Apart from this lapse of taste, however, the son of Sirach does his best for the learned faculty (Ecclus. 38.1–15). If we are ill, we are advised to send for the doctor, and to sacrifice to our Creator. Religion and science, between them, are to pull it off. We are reminded of the French curé who, for a very simple ailment, prescribed the recitation of three Paternosters with three Ave Marias, and the drinking of a bottle of olive oil.

We know that there is spiritual healing, and that the same complaint can quite often be usefully attacked from two ends at once, the bodily and the emotional. If a child is ill and cannot sleep, his mother can give him a drug, but then stroke his head and recit blessing-prayers. It will hardly do, however, to call the first part of the treatment human, and the second part divine. It is no more the act of God to soothe through words and handlings than it is to narcotize by chemical action. And as for the prayers, they may be effective; but suppose that, with the child in question, lullabies were to be found more so?

And even if the spiritual healing is genuinely spiritual and appeals to faith, do we not know that common sense will often rate it a poor second-best, compared with physical medicine? And it seems a most shocking conclusion, if we have recourse to God as a *pis aller*, or if (to turn it the other way round) those who rely on God, rather than on quinine, show themselves to be people of little sense.

The son of Sirach stands on better ground when he suggests that the doctor and his drugs may be instruments in the hands of God. And this surely is the essential point. Nothing but nonsense and blasphemy can ever result if we think of God's action as a rival to the action of any natural forces. God's will is the cause behind causes, and the force behind forces, not a cause or a force alternative to others. Even when God acts in our souls, he does not displace natural agents, he acts through them. For instance, when God speaks to us inwardly, he does so by acting in and through the natural processes of our thought. And since, in this case, it is ourselves, or something in ourselves, that he wields or uses, we can in a manner feel it, whereas we cannot feel God make the medicine work, for the medicine is no part of our personal being.

So when we pray, we put ourselves, our actions, and the whole setting of our lives, bodily or social, into almighty hands and pray that all may be instruments of the sovereign love. This is so, whether we are sick, or whether we are well; whether we pray for ourselves, or pray for our friends. We are making an act of faith in the master of all existences, and the wielder of all causes, believing that God will use us, our efforts and our skills, for his designs, and that a wisdom we often cannot interpret will always prevail.

39 · Temptations turn to Glory

Perhaps you have thought, reading the Gospel of Matthew, that the three temptations of Christ form a curiously isolated episode in the narrative (4.1–11). If you have thought anything like that, I will try to show you that you are wrong.

We will turn back to the previous page. John the Baptist has been telling the Pharisees not to rely on their physical descent for their membership in God's family, for, he says, God is able of these stones to raise up children unto Abraham. In the next section, Jesus comes to John's baptism. He undergoes it, and he knows in a moment that by the unspeakable act of God, he is himself the Son in whom the divine Father's heart delights, raised up, not of stone, indeed, but from the flesh of a village girl. He is swept away by the power of the Spirit into the wilderness, to be taught what this means. He is taught by temptations. The devil takes up where God left off. So you are the Son of God, are you? The Son of him, whose power could raise human beings from stones? If you are his Son, the power is yours; command that these stones become bread. But no:

to be the Son of God is not to set up as God on one's own account, and issue omnipotent commands; it is to listen for, and learn, and do, and feed upon the Father's will. Man shall not live by bread alone, but by every word that proceedeth out of the mouth of God. Very well, says the tempter; if it is a matter of drawing on God, draw on God: throw yourself from this height, if you are his Son, and feel his angels' shoulders under your feet. Ah, no, says Christ; it is no way to trust my Father, to set him tests. He told his children long ago, You shall not try things on with God your Lord. Then, says the tempter, since you will neither use your power, nor call in his, it seems you must enter into your inheritance by natural means. Nature is mastered by obeying her: the world is yours by right, bow to the spirit of the world, and it is yours in fact. No, says Christ, there is only one to whom I can bow. We have been commanded, Thou shalt love the Lord thy God, and him only serve. I can do nothing for you, said the devil, and departed.

Jesus went back into the world that was his, yet where he had no place to lay his head: as having nothing, and yet possessing all things; content to act by the will and power of God, as they should be revealed. And how were they revealed? Those very things which the devil put forward as temptations, the Father gave as mercies: the very things? – no, things a thousand times better. 'Command that these stones be made bread.' Not that, but – He took bread, and blessed it, and said, This is my body: not the bread that perishes, but the bread that sustains to everlasting life.

Cast thyself down: for it is written he shall give his angels charge concerning thee. Not that – but in due course he jumped the precipice of voluntary death: Father, into thy hands I commend my Spirit.

'Here are the kingdoms of the world and all the glory of them; they are yours, if you will fall down and worship me.' 'Get thee behind me, Satan.' But then, on the last page of the Gospel, Jesus appears to his disciples in glory; they fall down and worship him. And what does he say to them? 'All power is given unto me, in heaven and on earth.' In heaven, and on earth. We cannot have the earth, unless we have the heaven too. For we cannot possess anything, except by union with the dear love and will of him who made, and possesses and governs all things, whether they be in earth or in heaven. 'All things', says Christ's Apostle, 'are yours: for you are Christ's, and Christ is God's.'

40 · The Lamb of God

To draw together the sacrifice of Isaac and the supper of Christ requires no art of mine. Jesus came to Jerusalem to eat the Passover, and on the afternoon before they ate it, he and his disciples presented their lamb in the Temple where the priests cut its throat, caught the blood in a golden bowl and threw it against the base of the great altar. The blood of the lamb ran down through the holes in the rock on which the alter stood; and if you had asked the priests why that rock among all the rocks in the world drank the blood of sacrifice they would have answered that it was the mountain top on which Abraham had slaughtered the lamb provided by God in substitution for Isaac. We are all Isaac, the priest would have explained, we are all the seed of Abraham. And the blood of lambs is still accepted in place of us, here in God's holy mountain. The lambs are utterly given and devoted by the irrevocableness of death, but we, though bound hand and foot and given to God, are released that we may be a living sacrifice to him.

So then, in the place where the lamb had been substituted for Isaac, Jesus came to be substituted for the lamb. Isaac could not be actually sacrificed for many reasons, among them that his death would have been futile and immoral. But the reason that Genesis (ch. 22) suggests as making Isaac's sacrifice impossible is Isaac's innocence. 'My father.' 'Well, my son.' 'Here is the fire and the wood, but where is the lamb for sacrifice?' 'God will provide the lamb for sacrifice, my son.' What Abraham could not tell Isaac, God would not do to Isaac; Abraham lied, and had to lie, and God had to turn his lie into truth.'Do nothing to the lad; see, a ram behind caught by his horns in the thicket. Take him and sacrifice him in the stead of thy son.' Isaac was either too ignorant, or not ignorant enough. The lamb could die, because it was wholly ignorant; it would go cheerful and garlanded to an auspicious death. But it was intolerable that Isaac should die, knowing, and not knowing: led by the hand he most trusted in the world, into a trap which he could see with his eyes.

Jesus could die for the opposite reason to that which prevented the death of the boy: he was not ignorant, and if he trusted the hand that led him on, he trusted it without illusions. He saw that he must die and he saw why he must die, and he saw what lay beyond his death. Yet in a sense everyone, even Jesus, goes into death blindfold, for no one knows what it will be like. Nothing can be experienced in advance and least of all death. To know that you will be betrayed and deserted by your dearest friends is not to know how it will take you, and to know that you will be crucified is not to know what it will be like to be nailed up in the heat of the sun until your heart bursts.

There is, then, in Jesus' sacrifice the same clarity and the same blindness that there is in ours. In every least resignation of our will that we make to the will of God, every undertaking to submit to his pleasure and deny our own, there is illumination in the clarity of God's goodness and darkness in the mystery of his will. When God calls in the debt which your promise contracts to pay him, you do not yet know what payment will be like. You will say, 'I didn't know it would be like this' and you will be likely to go back on your word, forgetting that your salvation has been given you through your union with the sacrifice of Jesus Christ, for whom there was no going back. Death is death. When Jesus Christ gave his sacrifice to his disciples in bread and wine, he gave them death and resurrection in a sealed packet; sealed from them, for they had still to explore the riches of it; sealed from himself, for he had still to undergo it; yet well enough known to him for him to write the true description on the cover, and validly to will to his friends the thing that it contains. That will, made efficacious by the death of the testator, no authority in earth or heaven shall overthrow. Only let us pray for grace more fully to explore and more actively to use our inheritance, that whom we receive under a veil we may at length behold with open face, Jesus Christ our life and our everlasting joy.